GW00504847

TRAVELLERS

BALI &
LOMBOK

By
ALISON LEMER & JEROEN VAN MARLE

Written by Alison Lemer and Jeroen van Marle, updated by Jeroen van Marle
Original photography by Andy Day, Alison Lemer and Jeroen van Marle

Published by Thomas Cook Publishing
A division of Thomas Cook Tour Operations Limited.
Company registration no. 3772199 England
The Thomas Cook Business Park, Unit 9, Coningsby Road,
Peterborough PE3 8SB, United Kingdom
Email: books@thomascook.com, Tel: + 44 (0) 1733 416477
www.thomascookpublishing.com

Produced by Cambridge Publishing Management Limited
Burr Elm Court, Main Street, Caldecote CB23 7NU

ISBN: 978-1-84848-164-0

Series Editor: Maisie Fitzpatrick
Production/DTP Editor: Steven Collins

Printed and bound in Italy by: Printer Trento.

Front cover credits, front L–R: © Morandi Bruno/4Corners Images;
© Jon Arnold Images Ltd/Alamy; © Steve Allen Travel Photography
Back cover credits, back L–R: © Geoffrey Morgan/Alamy

Contents

Introduction

'Tropical', 'far-off', 'exotic' – the island of Bali has been capturing the imagination of Western travellers since the first foreign visitors stepped ashore almost a century ago. For many, the combination of sunny weather, wide beaches, a relaxed pace and inexpensive food and lodging is all they ask of a holiday spot, and for these alone can Bali stake its claim to the title of 'paradise'. But even all that is merely scratching the surface of what this little gem of an island has to offer.

Bali's natural gifts are not limited only to its coasts, although its multitudes of coral reefs are well known the world over for spectacular surfing, diving and snorkelling. Head away from the beaches and within minutes one can be immersed in a serene rural fantasy of stately palm trees, dense jungles, sweet-scented tropical flowers, cascading

A *barong*, or 'protective spirit'

terraces of silvery-green rice fields, and majestic volcanoes brooding quietly among the clouds.

But far more than these natural wonders, what makes Bali truly unique is its people, and the rich, centuries-old culture and history that play such a vivid and vital part of their lives. The devout Hinduism of the Balinese dictates that gods are everywhere on Bali, as are demons, and the multitudes of these supernatural beings must be continually worshipped, appeased and entertained, often at one of the tens of thousands of temples located all over the island. Much of classic Balinese artistic and crafts traditions – dancing, music, architecture, textiles, stone and woodcarvings, painting – stemmed from the desire to honour the gods with beauty, and visitors to Bali will see evidence of this everywhere, from the daily multitudes of pretty little offering baskets full of rice, sweets and flowers to the quiet grace of a temple's many-

Multi-tiered thatched *meru* towers are a feature of Balinese temples

tiered *meru* shrines or the intricately woven gold threads in the brocade costume of a *legong* dancer.

The amazing diversity of Bali's gifts, both natural and manufactured, means that the island really does have something to offer everyone: fantastic shopping and all-night parties in Kuta, luxurious pampering in Nusa Dua, family-friendly beaches at Sanur, traditional arts and crafts in Ubud, spectacular surfing and reef diving on the coasts, climbing sacred mountains or trekking through rainforests, quiet getaways to Lovina, Candi Dasa or Amed, wonderful food and accommodation to fit any budget, and, most of all, the warm hospitality of the Balinese people themselves. It's really no wonder they call it paradise.

Lombok

To the east of Bali lies Lombok, a much less-known and less-developed tourist destination, but easily reached and fascinating in its own way. Inhabited mainly by the Muslim Sasak people, but with a sizeable Hindu population, Lombok has a varied mix of sights, including thatched old mosques, elegant Balinese-style Hindu temples, traditional villages, verdant rice-paddy landscapes and Indonesia's second-highest volcano, although most visitors simply head for the beach resorts at Senggigi and Kuta (not to be confused with the town of the same name on Bali), or for relaxation and snorkelling and diving on one of the three Gili Islands off the northwest coast.

The islands: Bali

Bali is a small island located 8 degrees south of the equator, one of the more than 17,500 islands that make up the Republic of Indonesia. At only 140km (87 miles) in length east to west and 80km (50 miles) north to south, it has a total area of just 5,632sq km (2,175sq miles). Most of the 3.1 million people on Bali live in the southern, eastern and northern districts, while volcanoes dominate much of the centre and Bali's only national park takes up much of the far western area.

As part of the Pacific Ring of Fire, some of Bali's most enduring geographical features are the six volcanoes over 2,000m (6,500ft) high that range across it from east to west. The largest, Gunung (Mount) Agung, is 3,142m (10,308ft) high; the Balinese consider it the home of the deities, who may show their displeasure by causing a volcanic eruption, as happened in 1963, with

Bali is famous for its terraced rice paddies

devastating results. And yet for all their danger, the volcanoes are also gifts from the gods; their lava and ash have provided the lush and fertile soil that allows the Balinese to grow their crops, and their height attracts the rain clouds that fill the massive lakes at their feet – such as Danau (Lake) Batur – and provide the large amounts of water used for irrigation.

The biggest crop on Bali is rice, various species of which are grown for up to three yearly harvests in the cleverly terraced and irrigated rice paddies (*see pp72–3*) that cover 20 per cent of the island, mostly in the alluvial plains that lie south of the volcanoes. Other areas of the island, mainly the coastal areas to the north and east, do not get enough rainfall for rice and so dry-land crops are cultivated instead, such as grapes, coffee, fruits and vegetables, cocoa, spices, nuts, soya beans and chilli peppers. A few areas, such as the south's Bukit Badung or the rugged southwestern coast, are too arid to grow anything and were generally abandoned by the Balinese.

Off its coasts, Bali is surrounded by fringes of beautiful coral reefs, which give the island its fantastic surf breaks and dive sites and are also home to a variety of marine life. Traditionally only the poorer Balinese and those on the arid coasts turned to fishing, since on Bali the sea is considered the home of evil demons and is usually avoided (the Balinese have always focused inland, towards their holy mountains and

Tropical Bali is a study in blue and green

lakes). The culinary demands of the tourism and export industries, however, have created new markets for fish and seafood, and the tourists are certainly also happy to take advantage of Bali's white- and yellow-sand southern beaches (if perhaps not as much as their black-sand counterparts on the other coasts).

Much of the central areas are composed of lush monsoonal rainforests, home to many of the island's beautiful tropical flowers, which may be seen in offering baskets and tucked behind ears all over Bali. Such forests once covered more of the island but were cleared centuries ago to create land for the rice paddies.

The islands: Lombok

Bali's tourism development is a world away from Lombok, the slightly smaller island with 2.5 million inhabitants just 40km (25 miles) to the east. While Bali attracts over a million tourists a year, Lombok receives less than one-tenth of that amount. As a result, travelling on Lombok is quite a different experience – though the oft-heard statement that Lombok is 'Bali as it was 20 years ago' is somewhat unfair to an island that has a vibrant local culture all of its own.

North Lombok is dominated by massive Gunung Rinjani, Indonesia's second-highest volcano at 3,726m (12,224ft) and now the heart of a national park. Rain falls mainly on the southern slopes of the mountain, and as a result Central Lombok is dazzlingly green, densely populated and intensively farmed, with hundreds of villages such as Tetebatu set amid rice paddies and tobacco fields. North and east of the mountain, both water and people are much more scarce. Senggigi and the Gili Islands, along the rugged coast to the west of the volcano, boast fine white-sand beaches and are the focus of tourism on the island. South Lombok is a poor region, too far from the volcano to profit from the water runoff. The fishing village of Kuta is easily reached from the north and sees most tourists. There are some excellent beaches, hotels and restaurants near here, but otherwise the southern coastline is deliciously rugged and isolated, with roads deteriorating rapidly as you travel east or west from Kuta.

Sunrise over Gunung Rinjani volcano as seen from Gili Air, Lombok

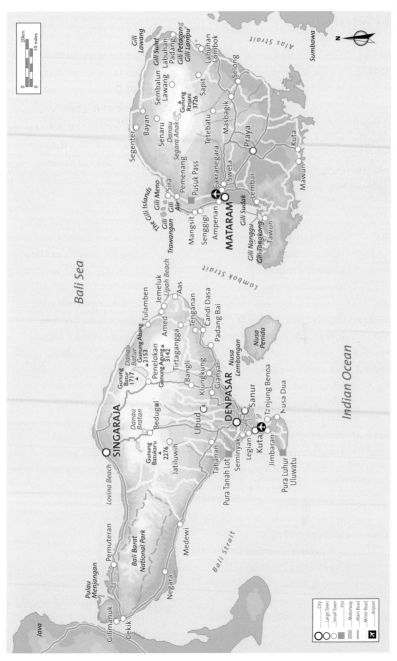

History

5000–3000 BC Austronesians from Taiwan and the Philippines migrate to Indonesian archipelago.

500 BC–AD 300 The Bronze Age flourishes in Bali.

1st–7th centuries Cultural influences from India take hold in Bali, spawning Buddhist ruling dynasties.

989 Buddhist Balinese King Udayana marries Hindu Javanese Princess Mahendradatta.

1011 Crown Prince Erlangga inherits the Javanese throne.

1049 Erlangga's death leads to civil war in Java. Bali becomes autonomous kingdom.

1284–92 Bali invaded by Singasari kingdom of Java, regaining independence six years later when Kublai Khan attacks Java.

1343 Majapahit kingdom of Java successfully colonises Bali, introducing the Hindu caste system.

1515 Islamic sultanates gain power in Java. Majapahit nobles, priests and artists flee to Bali.

1550 Successful military campaigns led by King Batu Renggong extend Balinese rule to western Java and the islands of Lombok and Sumbawa.

1597 First Dutch expedition lands in Bali.

1601–2 Bali agrees to formal trade relations with the Dutch, who form the Dutch East India Company (VOC).

1650–1799 Civil wars end unified Balinese rule. Regional kingdoms vie for control of Bali and Lombok. Dutch government takes control of Indonesian archipelago.

1846–9 Dutch forces invade northern Bali leading to first *puputan* ('mass ritual suicide'). Singaraja becomes colonial capital; kingdoms of southern and eastern Bali allowed to retain autonomy.

1904–9 Dutch invade remaining regional kingdoms; several courts commit *puputan*, giving the Dutch full control of Bali.

1917	Massive earthquake, plague and Spanish flu epidemic kill thousands of Balinese.
1942	Japan invades Indonesia, occupying Bali.
1945	Japan's surrender ends World War II. Sukarno declares Indonesia's independence.
1946	Balinese nationalist Ngurah Rai and his guerrilla fighters slaughtered by Dutch forces near Marga.
1949	The UN recognises Indonesia's independence; Dutch relinquish control.
1963	Gunung Agung erupts, killing thousands and destroying villages and crops.
1965	Alleged Communist coup fails in Indonesia; mass reprisal killings carried out nationwide.
1968	General Suharto replaces Sukarno as president.
1971	Indonesian government begins promoting Bali for international tourism. Within five years, visitor totals increase 3,000 per cent.
1986	Luxury resorts open at Nusa Dua.
1998	Economic crises and riots in Indonesia; Suharto resigns.
2001	Megawati Sukarnoputri, Sukarno's daughter, becomes first female president of Indonesia.
2002	Terrorists detonate a car bomb in Kuta, killing over 200 mostly foreign visitors and wounding 200 more.
2004	Megawati is defeated in direct presidential election by Susilo Bambang Yudhoyono.
2005	The tourism industry suffers again when bombs in Kuta and Jimbaran kill 20.
2007	The United Nations Climate Change Conference is held in Nusa Dua.
2008	Tourism numbers pick up as Bali and Lombok experience a boom year. The three Islamists from Java found guilty of the Kuta bombings are executed.
2009–11	In response to rising numbers of visitors, Bali's airport is set for a major two-year expansion project and work on a new airport on Lombok has started.

Politics

For centuries, the small island of Bali has been settled or manipulated by foreign interests, from the Hindu Majapahit rulers of Java to the colonial Dutch occupiers. Since the birth of the Republic of Indonesia in 1949, it has been one of the 33 provinces of the archipelago nation, and the only primarily Hindu province in the world's largest Muslim country.

Administration

The provincial capital is Denpasar, where Governor I Made Mangku Pastika, elected to his first term in 2008, resides. The island is divided into eight *kabupaten* ('districts'), which bear the names they had as the former kingdoms of Bali: Badung, Bangli, Buleleng, Gianyar, Jembrana, Karangasem, Klungkung and Tabanan. These are divided into 51 subdistricts

and then into *desas* ('villages'), which comprise the *dusun* ('hamlet') and the *banjar* ('village association') to which all adult married men in the village must belong. The *banjar* is responsible for various community and cultural services such as waste disposal and the organisation of weddings, cremations, festivals and the local *gamelan* orchestra.

Modern political history

As one of the jewels in the Dutch colonial crown, Bali found itself on the frontline of Indonesia's struggle for independence. The Japanese occupation during World War II saw the creation of guerrilla resistance groups like the People's Military Force, led by I Gusti Ngurah Rai. After Japan's surrender, these nationalist groups resisted the re-establishment of the Dutch administration. Ngurah Rai and 94 men were slaughtered by Dutch forces at Marga, in Tabanan, on 20 November 1946. A national hero, Ngurah Rai is

A political palm tree sports a local election poster

memorialised in a monument at Marga, the name of Denpasar's bypass road and the name of Bali's international airport.

Independence in 1949 did not ease Bali's political problems. In 1963, the eruption of Gunung Agung led to the relocation of thousands as part of Indonesia's much-disputed transmigration policies, laying the groundwork for the Hindu Balinese people's distrust of the Muslim-dominated government. In 1965, an attempted coup led to political purges across the nation and the murders of up to 100,000 Balinese (and 50,000 more on Lombok). Three years later, military leader Suharto replaced Sukarno as president.

Recent politics

Suharto retired in 1998 after three decades in power, and his unpopular vice-president B J Habibie served just 18 months after the MPR (the higher legislature) fought his bid for the next election. In 1999, the MPR convened to elect the new president. The secular, democratic PDI-P party had earned 33 per cent of the votes, and its popular leader Megawati Sukarnoputri, daughter of Sukarno and beloved by the Balinese, was expected to win. But political intrigues gave the office to Abdurrahman Wahid, of the Muslim PKB party. Angry demonstrations took place across Bali and Java, and Megawati was quickly elected vice-president to quell unrest. The MPR removed the

ineffectual Wahid in 2001 and Megawati became president. Disillusionment with her leadership eventually led to the departure of PDI-P party members (including her two sisters), and in 2004, Indonesia's first-ever direct presidential elections saw Megawati lose decisively to Democratic Party candidate Susilo Bambang Yudhoyono (known as SBY), who was able to earn the popular vote even on Bali.

The Balinese now have high hopes that the new governor I Made Mangku Pastika will clamp down on corruption and pay more attention to development and environmental issues. Pastika is the former chief of police who helped capture the Bali bombers, and he was elected governor of the island in 2008.

Bali's small Muslim population prays at mosques like this one

Trouble in paradise

For decades Bali has been famous as a tourist's dream, with its tropical climate and beautiful countryside, its cultural sights and recreational activities, and its welcoming natives and low prices. But recent terrorist attacks have since threatened to turn that dream into a nightmare.

The Memorial Plaza for the victims of the 2002 bombings in Kuta

The night of 12 October 2002 was much like any Saturday night in the thriving tourist centre of Kuta. Bars and nightclubs on the main road Jalan Legian were filled with crowds of young visitors from all over the world – particularly from nearby Australia – enticed by the cheap alcohol and an all-night party atmosphere. At 11.05pm, a suicide bomber set off a small explosive in Paddy's Irish Bar, sending frightened, injured patrons fleeing into the street. Just 15 seconds later, a massive car bomb – weighing close to 1,000kg (2,200lb) – exploded in front of the Sari Club, a packed nightclub located across the street.

What had only seconds before been a lively street filled with young party-goers was now a scene of horrendous carnage. Burned corpses and body parts lay scattered as fires raged among the debris of the surrounding buildings, all destroyed by an explosion so fierce it left a crater 1m (40in) deep and blew out windows in a 500m (1,640ft) radius. The final death toll was 202 people from 22 countries, almost half of them Australian, with a significant number of Britons and Indonesians; another 200 were badly wounded. The local hospital was overwhelmed, and many victims had to be airlifted to Australia.

Worldwide reactions of shock and grief were swift and profound, especially in Bali and Australia, who considered the attacks 'their 9/11'. The idea of Bali as a pleasure-filled paradise far from the world's ills was shattered, and many Balinese wondered if the attacks were divine retribution for encouraging foreign hedonism on their shores. Tourism plunged overnight, taking with it the Balinese economy.

The Indonesian government soon captured several suspects belonging to Jemaah Islamiyah, a militant group with ties to Al-Qaeda and dedicated to the establishment of Islamic states across Southeast Asia. Five men were tried for the worst act of terror in Indonesian history, with four receiving death sentences.

Bali's tourism industry slowly recovered, only to suffer another setback in October 2005 when three suicide bombs exploded in Kuta and Jimbaran, claiming 20 lives and injuring over 100, mostly Indonesians. Since then, security measures have been tightened and tourist numbers have again risen, with a record number of 2 million tourists visiting in 2008 and a flurry of investments in the tourism sector.

A memorial plaza at the site of the bombings commemorates the victims – for Bali, the dream of paradise has been forever altered.

Culture

Besides sun, sand and sea, Bali is probably best known for its vibrant, multifarious artistic culture. Javanese influences from the 14th-century Majapahit kingdom played an early role, but new styles have developed over time, especially in the past century and often from exposure to expatriate Western artists. The vitality of Balinese culture today is due in part to the Dutch, whose colonial policies and early 20th-century tourism encouraged its preservation and development.

Architecture

Balinese architecture has strong Hindu-Buddhist and Javanese influences. Both family compounds and temples (*see pp84–5*) are laid out in relation to the island's sacred mountains and the sea, and the concept of the duality underlying all of creation – good and

evil, night and day, female and male – is also significant. The most commonly seen structures are the *bale* (raised, open-sided platforms with a roof, also popular across Southeast Asia), which are built for various purposes, such as sitting, eating, conducting ceremonies or storage space, and the temple *meru*,

A *bale* structure in the courtyard of Puri Anyar palace

thatched towers with an odd number of tiers from 3 to 11 (depending on the temple's status) that represent Mount Meru, the sacred Hindu mountain where the gods reside. Temples also feature distinctive split-towered gateways between their courtyards; known as *candi bentar*, they symbolise the world's dual nature and will supposedly crash together should a demon try to enter the temple.

Handicrafts

Skilled Balinese artisans are especially known for their woven cloth, wood and stone carvings, fine metalwork and a number of different painting styles (*see pp62–3*). The Gianyar district, home to the cultural centre of Ubud, produces the highest-quality crafts on Bali (*see p56*).

In textiles, the Balinese are particularly known for their masterful ikat-style cloth, called *endek*, in which the weft (horizontal) threads are skilfully dyed before weaving to produce intricate patterns in the finished cloth. Even more complicated is the double-ikat style, known on Bali as *gringsing*, in which both the weft and warp (vertical) threads are dyed before weaving; a single piece can take up to one year to complete. *Gringsing* is produced only in the village of Tenganan (*see pp78–9*).

Stone carving was developed for the elaborate adornments needed for the many temples and palaces – baroque, fanciful designs depicting gods and

A woodcarving from the village of Mas

demons, heroes and warriors, and scenes from everyday life. Woodcarvers create all sorts of statues and figures, large and small, holy and secular, as well as architectural pieces for use in family compounds and the gilded wooden cases for *gamelan* instruments.

Gold and silversmiths once supplied the jewellery for Balinese royalty, but now the tourist trade is their main market, for which they create pieces in a number of styles from traditional to more modernist designs. Other metalsmiths working in iron and bronze produce the highly specialised *keris* (Balinese dagger) and *gamelan* instruments.

Performing arts

Many forms of dance, drama and puppetry were developed for religious ceremonies, although in recent years secular forms have evolved for tourist performances. Many recount stories from the two great Hindu religious epics, the *Ramayana* and the *Mahabharata*, or are based on other Hindu or Balinese legends like the malevolent widow-witch Rangda.

Dancers are arrayed in magnificent costumes, often made of *songket* (a gold or silver brocade), with elaborate headdresses and gold jewellery. Masks are often used, especially for demon or animal characters such as the two-man *barong*, a protective spirit (often in the form of a lion) that fights the Rangda. Many of the styles use precise gestures with folding fans and the fingers, eyes and head, such as the 18th-century *legong*, formerly performed for royal courts, in which three young women

Two male dancers are required to dance the *barong* character

dance with tightly synchronised movements. The well-known *kecak*, or 'monkey dance', has a troupe of at least 50 men chanting and moving in unison and was developed by a famous Balinese dancer in the 1930s using earlier traditions of ritual trance dances.

Wayang kulit ('shadow puppetry') is another Javanese-inspired art form used to tell the stories of brave heroes and virtuous maidens from Hindu epics. The puppets are made from leather parchment, cut with intricate patterns and painted with gold leaf, and manipulated by thin rods attached to the joints. The *dalang* ('puppeteer') moves them under a lamp behind a stretched white sheet to display the shadows to the audience.

Dances and puppet shows are always accompanied by a *gamelan* orchestra, which uses metal xylophones with resonating bamboo bases and various gongs, drums and flutes to create the highly singular, rather jangly *gamelan* style. Each village owns a complete set, sometimes for up to 40 players, and as there are no standard musical scales, each instrument is built and tuned specifically to the rest of its ensemble.

Lombok

While similar to Bali in some respects, Lombok has a culture all of its own. Traditional music and dance are strongly linked to the local Sasak Muslim and Hindu religions, and as the tourism industry hasn't yet organised tourist performances on the scale of Bali, religious festivals and ceremonies are your best chance of witnessing a performance. You'll often have to ask around to see if there's anything on in the area.

Travelling around Lombok, you're quite likely to come across wedding processions (among other events), which take place regularly and are often quite public happenings, even blocking traffic for a while. Both the bride and groom will have a *gendang beleq* (literally 'big drum') band at their disposal, which slowly and very noisily makes its way through the village, meeting up with its counterpart and then continuing to the site of the wedding ceremony. *Gendang beleq* groups can have up to 30 musicians with drums and cymbals, and sometimes also have dancers. As on Bali, *gamelan* music is quite popular at festivals, often accompanied by *gendang beleq.*

Crafts are an essential part of life in Lombok, providing extra income for rural families during lulls in the agricultural season. Lombok specialities include the characteristic brown pottery that's decorated with rattan and even broken eggshells, woven ikat and *songket* fabrics, basketware items of bamboo or rattan, and carved wooden masks and furniture. Several villages dedicated to a particular craft can be visited on Lombok, and tourists are always welcome to have a look at the manufacturing process.

Women bake clay pots in Masbagik Timur crafts village on Lombok

Festivals and events

An estimated 1.5 million tourists visit Bali each year, so it's little wonder that the island has become home to a number of annual festivals and events. For obvious reasons, many occur during peak and high tourist seasons, so be sure to book your hotel room well in advance if planning your trip around a specific event. For religious festivals, see pp22–3.

Arts
Bali Arts Festival
The biggest cultural event in Bali is a massive, month-long celebration of Balinese arts, with events held every day in Denpasar. Performers from all over Bali come to display their music, singing and dance skills; visitors can also enjoy food, handicrafts and historical exhibitions. Held June–July.
www.baliartsfestival.com

Ubud Writers and Readers Festival
The cultural heart of Bali beats a little stronger each September at the Ubud Writers Festival. Each features a different theme, internationally known authors, and six days of readings, workshops, lunches, book launches, poetry slams and children's events.
www.ubudwritersfestival.com

Culture
Chinese New Year
The Chinese population of Bali is estimated at around 150,000.

Descendants of one of the oldest communities, in Tanjung Benoa, are believed to have migrated to Bali in the 7th century. Visitors from all over Asia join them in celebrating the lunar-based Chinese New Year, with festivals all over the island that include parades, dances, firework displays and other cultural events. Held in January or February (changes yearly).

Kuta Karnival
A nine-day public celebration that includes competitions in everything from surfing and football to beach volleyball and kite flying, as well as parades, food and music festivals, nightly dances and even a dog show. Check the website for the dates.
www.kutakarnival.com

Sport
Indonesian Surfing Championships
Various events on the Indonesian Pro Surfing Tour are held yearly at Bali,

home to some of the world's most famous rips and breaks. The tour is sponsored by some of the biggest names in the industry (Rip Curl, Quiksilver and Billabong, to name a few) and top surfers from Indonesia and the rest of the world compete. Various dates and locations. *www.isctour.com*

Wismilak International

The biggest women's tennis tournament in Southeast Asia (an official WTA event), Wismilak attracts top-ranked players from all over the world – former number-ones Lindsay Davenport and Svetlana Kuznetsova were some recent champions. Held in September in Nusa Dua.

Lombok

Lombok's best festivals take place during the tourist high season. Each April, the *Gendang Beleq* **Festival** in Senggigi sees musicians with large drums and cymbals bash out high-speed rhythms to which dancers frenetically move. Several bands parade and compete during the week-long festival along the resort's main street.

Also in April, the extremely popular *Male'an Sampi* cattle race festival is held in the waterlogged rice paddies near Narmada.

The **Senggigi Festival** is held in the second or third week of July to promote tourism on Lombok. The week-long festival features music, dance, crafts demonstrations, a cultural parade and *peresean* stick fighting competitions.

A colourful *barong* kite is ready for the next kite festival

Religious festivals

Agama Hindu Dharma, the type of Hinduism practised on Bali, is a dynamic and intrinsic part of Balinese life. Offerings to the gods are laid out on pavements and in shrines several times each day, and various religious ceremonies are held regularly, including a three-day anniversary celebration (*odalan*) for each temple, calculated according to the *pawukon*, a lunar-based calendar of 210 days.

Your trip will most likely coincide with at least one ceremony somewhere nearby; visitors are generally welcome to watch respectfully, so enquire at a tourist office for local schedules. Massive, island-wide public holidays are also held every year, with the Balinese busily preparing for them weeks in advance.

The most sacred Balinese holiday is *Galungan*, a ten-day festival celebrating the victory of good over evil, when the gods descend to earth and the deified souls of ancestors return to visit their families. Temples are gaily decorated with *penjor*, bamboo poles hung with offerings, and animals are slaughtered for ritual feasts. Balinese return to their ancestral homes on this day to celebrate with their families, praying to and entertaining the spirits of their ancestors. The remaining days are spent visiting friends, picnicking and generally enjoying the festive atmosphere until *Kuningan*, the final day, on which family members reunite to bid farewell to their ancestors' souls as they return to heaven.

The other main annual festival is *Nyepi*, the Balinese New Year, held usually in March or April. For several

Chickens are dyed bright colours for religious ceremonies

days beforehand, preparations are carried out and religious objects purified at sacred springs or sea temples. On the night before, *Pengrupukan*, the Balinese chase away evil spirits by noisily hitting drums, gongs, cymbals and bamboo tubes, while huge papier-mâché demons (*ogoh-ogoh*) are paraded through the streets and burned in effigy. On *Nyepi* itself, however, everyone on Bali spends the entire day in total silence, to fool demons into thinking the island has been abandoned and should be passed over. People sit quietly indoors with lights kept low, and pray or meditate. Village guards patrol to enforce these restrictions. (Exceptions are made for medical emergencies or women in childbirth.) Airlines are not allowed to fly to or from Bali, and tourists are asked to stay inside their hotels for the entire day, although hotel facilities are allowed to stay open to serve them.

Lombok

Lombok's most famous festival, *Bau Nyale* (see p111), takes place on Kuta's beaches in February or March, when thousands of spawning nyale sea worms are caught and eaten. Also in March, one day before the Hindu New Year, the *Tawur Kesanga* Festival and *Ogoh-Ogoh* Parade sees a statue of Bhuta Kalla, representing negative power, spun round and cremated. Around October, Lombok's Muslims pray, eat and go to the beach to celebrate *Lebaran Topat* seven days after the last day of Ramadan fasting. In November, thousands of Hindu pilgrims climb up to Gunung Rinjani's sacred crater lake to give thanks for the blessings of the past year in the *Nguturang Pekelam* Festival. The *Perang Topat* rice cake war, held in November, is perhaps Lombok's best festival, when Sasaks and Hindus gather at Pura Lingsar temple to give thanks for a good harvest and throw *topat* rice cakes at each other.

TEMPLE ETIQUETTE

There are 20,000 temples on Bali, so chances are good that you'll visit at least one, and perhaps even witness a ceremony. Follow these guidelines to avoid causing offence:

- Dress modestly and always wear a sarong and sash at temples. If you don't have your own, you'll need to hire them.
- If there is no fixed admission charge, it's still mandatory to 'donate' when entering most Hindu temples on Bali and Lombok; the fee is basically up to you, usually Rp5,000–10,000.
- People with open wounds or menstruating women are forbidden in temples, as shedding blood makes someone 'impure'.

If attending a ceremony:

- Don't climb or sit higher than the priest or table of offerings.
- Don't walk in front of people who are praying, or take their photo – and never use a flash.

Highlights

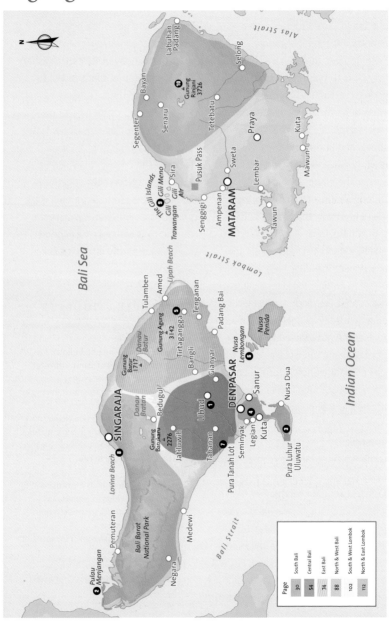

Bali Sea

Alas Strait

Labuhan
Padang

Selong

Bayan

Gunung
Rinjani
3726

Segenter

Senaru

Tetebatu

Praya

Kuta

Pusuk Pass

Sweta

The Gill Islands

Gili Meno

Gili
Sira
Air

Lembar

Mawun

Gili
Trawangan

Ampenan

MATARAM

Senggigi

Tawun

Lombok Strait

Tulamben

Amed

Lipah Beach

Tenganan

Gunung Agung
3142

Tirtagangga

Padang Bai

Nusa
Penida

Gunung
Batur
1717

Danau
Batur

Bangli

Gianyar

Nusa
Lembongan

Danau
Bratan

Bedugul

Ubud

DENPASAR

Sanur

SINGARAJA

Nusa Dua

Gunung Batukaru
2276

Seminyak

Legian

Jatiluwih

Kuta

Lovina Beach

Tabanan

Indian Ocean

Pemuteran

Pura Tanah Lot

Pura Luhur
Uluwatu

Pulau
Menjangan

Bali Barat
National Park

Medewi

Bali Strait

Negara

Page	
30	South Bali
54	Central Bali
74	East Bali
88	North & West Bali
102	South & West Lombok
112	North & East Lombok

① Ubud A vibrant arts scene, handmade traditional crafts, a delightful countryside and nearby recreational activities make this cultural centre of Bali worth an extended visit (*see pp57–61*).

② Pulau Menjangan The spectacular coral reefs and tropical fish off this tiny island offer some of the best diving and snorkelling on Bali (*see pp90–91*).

③ Pura Luhur Uluwatu Even the sunset crowds can't ruin the stunning sea views from the cliffs at one of Bali's holiest temples (*see pp45–6*).

④ Nightlife in South Bali Bali comes alive at night in the boisterous bars of Kuta, chilled-out lounges of Legian and sophisticated nightclubs of Seminyak (*see pp36–41*).

⑤ Tirtagangga Water Palace The elegant pools at this aquatic retreat surrounded by valleys of rice fields and distant mountains evoke the splendour of Bali's proud royal past (*see p80*).

⑥ Nusa Lembongan Known for its seaweed farms, this relaxed island has lovely cove beaches, affordable resorts and some serious surfing and diving spots (*see pp86–7*).

⑦ Pura Tanah Lot The starkly beautiful coastal location of this sacred sea temple makes it the most photographed holy site in Bali (*see p68*).

⑧ Relaxing in Lovina Hanging out at this low-key beach resort on the north coast is a welcome respite from the ultra-touristy areas down south (*see pp92–3*).

⑨ The Gili Islands Just off Lombok's western coast, these three small and quiet islands are ideal for sunbathing, snorkelling and diving – you'll probably see turtles – or simply lazing around (*see pp107–109*).

⑩ Gunung Rinjani National Park Hike to the crater rim or peak of Lombok's soaring volcano, or just enjoy the cool climate and light walks around the villages on its flanks (*see pp115–17*).

Tetebatu's rice fields and palm trees form a perfect frame for Gunung Rinjani volcano

Suggested itineraries

Bali and Lombok have a fantastic range of opportunities for artistic and cultural expeditions, fine dining and carousing, inexpensive shopping, recreational activities and just plain lazing around, so no matter what your holiday inclinations are or how much time you have, it's not difficult to come up with an itinerary that will suit everyone in your party. The small size of each island makes covering a lot of ground quite easy, so even visitors with shorter holidays can attempt a wide range of experiences.

BALI
Long weekend

If you have only a few days budgeted for Bali, your best bet will be to find accommodation in the major tourist centres of the south. If you simply want some relaxing luxury for a few days, pamper yourself with a stay at one of the lush resorts in Nusa Dua, Tanjung Benoa or Seminyak. If you crave a bit more excitement and want to stay somewhere with a beautiful surfing beach, bustling streets, plenty of restaurants and shops and a dynamic nightlife, find a hotel or nice *losmen* in Kuta – or Legian, if you want to avoid the younger crowds and prefer something more upscale but still close to the action. From all of those places, you can easily arrange an afternoon visit to Denpasar or day trips to must-see sights like the temples at Tanah Lot and Uluwatu. Also worthwhile is a day trip

Tirtagangga Water Palace, East Bali

The lagoon at Candi Dasa

to Ubud to explore the art museums and craft-making villages nearby, perhaps even catching one of the numerous traditional dance performances given every night of the week.

One week

With one week you could choose to spend a few days each in two different areas, perhaps starting somewhere down south for the 'classic' Bali experience of white-sand beaches and dining and drinking bargains, with a day trip to Tabanan to see Pura Tanah Lot and the beautiful rice paddies of Jatiluwih. Afterwards you can transfer to Ubud for a few days to immerse yourself in cultural activities, ancient sights such as Gunung Kawi and Yeh Pulu, and inland recreational activities like rice-paddy trekking or river rafting.

If you prefer coastal areas, you can instead opt for the quieter, less-visited areas like Lovina up north or Candi Dasa to the east. Lovina has a relaxed social atmosphere and is a good base for snorkelling or diving trips to Pulau Menjangan or Tulamben or a hike through Bali Barat National Park, while quiet Candi Dasa gives you easy access to the majestic volcano Gunung Agung and its holy temples, the traditional village of Tenganan and the water palace at Tirtagangga, and diving, snorkelling or surfing at Nusa Lembongan, just off the east coast.

For a real contrast, try a few lively days in Kuta followed by a trip to Lombok's relaxed Gili Islands. Head for Gili Trawangan if you still want a nightly social scene, or the less-frequented Gilis Air or Meno for some tropical tranquillity.

Two or more weeks

With a trip of several weeks, you can see a great deal of Bali and take some time to visit Lombok as well. Start off with a few days enjoying the vibrant tourist areas of South Bali and then move on to explore Ubud and the picturesque rice paddies of Tabanan. Charter a private driver to take you to Lovina, stopping off on the way in Bedugul for a visit to Bali's Botanical Gardens and the lovely lake temple, Pura Ulan Danu Bratan. Enjoy a few relaxing days in Lovina, with day trips for snorkelling in Pulau Menjangan or seeing the hot springs and temples around Singaraja and the north coast. From the north you can head to the east inland to see the venerated Gunung Batur and Gunung Agung. You can stay in the area or just pass through on your way to the east coast, where you can choose to stay a few days in the quieter areas of Amed or Candi Dasa

(or both). From there it's a short drive to Padang Bai, where you can take a tourist boat directly to Lombok to spend a few days in the unspoiled Gili Islands. You can take a boat to the mainland and a taxi to the airport to catch the 20-minute flight back to Bali, winding up your last day or two by buying gifts for everyone back home in the art markets and souvenir shops of Kuta. If you have more time and the inclination to explore Lombok further, read on for some suggestions.

LOMBOK

Lombok's small size and good road network make the island perfect for both short and longer trips. Some people visit the sights on day trips from Senggigi, but for a less rushed

The classical *legong* dance can be seen in Ubud, the cultural heart of Bali

Pristine Mawun beach west of Kuta on Lombok

holiday and more local insight, it's recommended to rent a car and spend a night or two at each destination. Public transport is patchy away from the city and tourist resorts, and having a rental car gives you the flexibility to explore the island on your own terms and at your preferred pace.

Long weekend

A short stay on Lombok is perhaps best spent relaxing on the beaches of either the Gili Islands or those near Kuta in the south. More active travellers could base themselves in the cooler air of Tetebatu and explore the surrounding rice paddies and crafts villages.

One week

With a week on Lombok you'll be able to spend a day exploring the sights in and around Mataram, relax on the Gili Islands or Kuta beaches, and still have time to do a trip to Tetebatu or short hikes around Senaru or up to the Gunung Rinjani crater rim.

Two or more weeks

Lombok's most attractive sights can all be explored on a two-week trip. After a few days of relaxing, snorkelling or diving on one of the Gili Islands, visit Senaru to do walks in the surroundings and perhaps hike up to Gunung Rinjani's lake or summit. Visit Sembalun Lawang to the east of the mountain for the village walks and take the pass road across to Tetebatu. From here, it's a pleasant downhill ride to Kuta on the south coast, where dazzling white sandy bays await.

South Bali

Once a barely settled expanse of uncultivable land considered the province of demons, south Bali is now the most populous part of the island, despite being only one-tenth of the total area. As well as home to Bali's administrative capital, Denpasar, it's the main draw for tourists due to the proximity of the airport to the tourist conurbation of Kuta, Legian and Seminyak and beach resorts of Nusa Dua and Tanjung Benoa. Quieter areas such as Sanur and Jimbaran are attractive alternatives.

The majority of foreign visitors make South Bali their first stop, and many of them never feel the need to go elsewhere – little wonder, considering that this area has not only the best beaches, water sports and surfing, but the most hotels, restaurants, bars, nightclubs and luxury resorts. The lively pace of the tourist enclaves here may not be for everyone, but if your holiday objective can be defined as 'fun in the sun', South Bali has everything you need.

Orientation

The main tourist area of Kuta (including its immediate neighbours Legian and Seminyak) sprawls along the western coast of South Bali, just 3km (1³/₄ miles) north of Ngurah Rai International Airport. Seven kilometres (4¹/₃ miles) to the northeast of Kuta is the bustling hub of Denpasar, with Sanur located on the eastern coast just to the south of it. A narrow spit of land leads from Kuta to the peninsula of Bukit Badung, the southernmost tip of Bali, home to the Nusa Dua and Tanjung Benoa resort areas in the east and a number of surfing beaches, Pura Luhur Uluwatu temple, and Jimbaran in the west.

DENPASAR

Bali's largest city has a population of over 400,000 and a sprawling network of streets bustling with motorbikes and other traffic, centred around a peaceful, grassy square that commemorates one of Bali's bloodiest historical events. Although it's not considered a tourist attraction per se, Denpasar has a few attractions worth a day trip, including the largest culture and history museum in Bali and some busy marketplaces and commercial districts. As an escape from tourist-centred Kuta, it will also give you a better idea of actual city life in Indonesia.

History

Before the arrival of the Dutch, Denpasar was known as Badung, governing city of the regency of the same name. In

1906, Badung fell to the Dutch with the mass suicide of the king and his court. After Bali won independence from the Dutch with the founding of Indonesia in 1949, the capital was moved from the northern city of Singaraja to Badung and renamed Denpasar.

Orientation

The historical centre is located at Puputan Square, adjacent to the four-headed statue at the intersection of two of Denpasar's main roads, Jalan Gajah Mada and Jalan Veteran. Most of the sights of interest to visitors are ranged around this square, including the Bali Museum and Pura Jagatnatha to the east and the city's markets and commercial streets to the west and south.

Alun-alun Puputan (Puputan Square)

This open expanse of grass is a popular spot for locals to relax in on evenings and weekends, as well as a verdant memorial to the downfall of one of

the last kings of Bali, whose palace once stood just to the north. On 20 September 1906, with Dutch forces massed in far superior strength outside, the king of Badung ordered the palace destroyed and assembled in the field with up to 2,000 of his subjects dressed in their finest attire and armed with *keris* (Balinese daggers) and spears, readying themselves for a *puputan*, a fight to the death. The Dutch tried in vain to negotiate a surrender, but were forced to shoot when the Balinese advanced. Those not struck down by bullets finished themselves or others with their blades, and soon the field was strewn with bodies. A large bronze statue depicting three Balinese with weapons stands at the northern end of the square, and a formal ceremony is held here every year on the anniversary.
Corner of Jl Udayana and Jl Surapati.

Bali Museum

The premier tourist sight in Denpasar, the Bali Museum offers a good introduction to Balinese history and culture, presented in four wings built in traditional regional styles. Exhibits on display include some original photographs taken at the 1906 *puputan*, traditional paintings and carvings, examples of Balinese textiles, ritual items from Balinese ceremonial life, and costumes and masks from different performing arts.
Jl Mayor Wisnu. Tel: (0361) 222 860. Open: Mon–Thur 8am–3pm, Fri 8am–noon. Closed: Sat & Sun. Admission charge.

Pasar Badung and Pasar Kumbasari

These two traditional markets are located on either side of the Badung river in huge multi-storey buildings, every nook and cranny crammed with an amazing array of foodstuffs and handicrafts. Local women will try to guide you to various stalls (expecting a service fee), but wandering the aisles yourself will be just as rewarding. Pasar Badung, east of the river, is primarily for produce, spices, meats and housewares, while Pasar Kumbasari is a traditional *pasar seni* ('art market') selling clothes, carvings, paintings, home décor and other souvenir and gift options.
Near the corner of Jl Gajah Mada and Jl Sulawesi. Open: 8am–5pm.

Pura Jagatnatha

Immediately to the east of Puputan Square is this state temple, built in 1953

WHAT'S IN A NAME?

Meet enough Balinese by name and you may start getting déjà vu. That's because Balinese tradition strictly dictates the naming of children according to social caste and birth order. For members in the *sudra* ('commoner') caste – who make up more than 90 per cent of the population – first-born children are always named 'Wayan', 'Putu' or 'Gede'; second-born, 'Made' or 'Kadek'; third, 'Nyoman' or 'Komang'; and the fourth, 'Ketut'. Any further children and the order starts again from the beginning. These names are assigned regardless of gender, so you'll often see prefixes of 'I' (for men) or 'Ni' (for women), such as 'I Wayan' or 'Ni Ketut'.

and dedicated to Sanghyang Widi Wasa, the Supreme Deity who manifests as the many gods and goddesses of Balinese Hinduism. The outer wall of the middle courtyard contains carvings with scenes from the *Ramayana* and the *Mahabharata*, the two central epics of Hindu morality. Festivals are held at the temple at every full and new moon. You can find a schedule of these at the Denpasar Tourist Office located directly across the street.

Pura Jagatnatha. Jl Mayor Wisnu. Tel: (0361) 253 300. Open: daylight hours. Admission by donation.

Denpasar Tourist Office *Jl Surapati 7. Tel: (0361) 234 569.*
Open: Mon–Thur 7.30am–1.30pm, Fri 7.30am–1pm.

Pura Maospahit

The oldest temple in the city, dating back to the late 14th century when the Javanese kingdom of Majapahit conquered Bali and instituted Hinduism. An earthquake in 1917 caused considerable damage but the temple was reconstructed.

Jl Sutomo. Open: daylight hours. Admission by donation.

A courtyard at the Bali Museum

Walk: Denpasar

This walk through the centre of Bali's largest city touches on both its historical past and its commercial present, including a museum, a temple and some busy craft and food markets.

Approximately 2km (1¹/₄ miles). Allow 1–3 hours, depending on museum, temple and market visits.

Begin at the Inna Bali Hotel on Jl Veteran.

1 Inna Bali Hotel
The first hotel in Bali, built in 1927 by the Dutch for the burgeoning tourist trade. Once a luxurious haven for Westerners, these days its genteel but slightly shabby facilities are more popular with Indonesians.
With the main entrance behind you, turn right and walk south to the roundabout.

2 Catur Mukha statue
This busy roundabout is the official centre of Denpasar. The four-faced statue in the middle depicts the Hindu gods of the cardinal points: Wisnu (Vishnu) faces north; Brahma, south; Iswara (Ishvara), east; and Mahadewa, west.
Walk east and cross over Jl Surapati to the grassy square of Alun-alun Puputan.

3 Alun-alun Puputan
This public park, considered the heart of Denpasar, commemorates the mass suicide that took place here on 20 September 1906 by the last king of Badung and his subjects (*see pp32–3*).

Across Jalan Surapati is the official residence of the governor of Bali, located on the former site of the king's palace.
Continue walking east across the park to the temple.

4 Pura Jagatnatha
This state temple was built in 1953 to honour the supreme Hindu god, Sanghyang Widi Wasa (*see pp32–3*).
Walk south along the eastern side of the park to the adjacent museum.

5 Bali Museum
Bali's largest cultural museum is worth a visit for its picturesque courtyards and informative historical exhibits (*see p32*).
Exiting the museum, turn left and walk south to Jl Sugianyar. Turn right and walk west, crossing Jl Udayana and Jl Sumatra until the road ends at Jl Sulawesi. Turn right and walk north.

6 Jalan Sulawesi
This bustling commercial street is known as the main clothing and textile

street in Denpasar. Have a browse through some of the shops or continue to the Pasar Badung.

Walk north on Jl Sulawesi to the market on your left.

7 Pasar Badung

The largest traditional produce market in Bali is located in a huge four-storey building surrounded by a maze of courtyard stalls. Avoid the women who will try to guide you around for a fee and instead take a wander through the seemingly infinite rows of fruit, vegetables, seafood, meat, spices and flowers. The art market on the top floor sells sarongs, art, handicrafts, clothing and more.

Walk across the Badung River via the bridge to the Pasar Kumbasari.

8 Pasar Kumbasari

Just across Denpasar's rather unappealing river is a multi-floored art market, with hundreds more stalls crammed with housewares, woodcarvings, clothing, paintings, ceremonial objects and other gifts and souvenirs. There are also some inexpensive cafés to stop at for a meal.

Jl Gajah Mada is at the northern end of the market. Turn right on it and walk east to reach the Catur Mukha statue. Taxis can be hailed anywhere along this street.

Walk: Denpasar

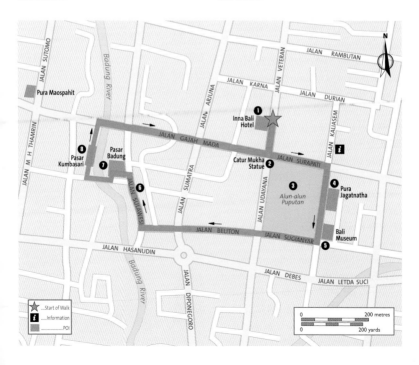

KUTA, LEGIAN AND SEMINYAK

Possibly the most famous tourist resort in Bali, the densely packed Kuta area is almost universally either loved or despised, crass and commercial, exciting and cosmopolitan, bursting with both the best and worst of recreational excess. And yet the respite of Kuta's broad, soft beach, with its full-bodied waves so beloved by surfers, is just steps beyond the rows of endless shops and bars and restaurants. For the combination of a picturesque seaside, fantastic food and shopping and a pulsating nightlife – not to mention the incredible sunsets – Kuta simply can't be beaten.

History

For most of Bali's history, the area around Kuta was considered by the Balinese to be a wasteland – the earth useless for crops, the surf too rough for fishing, the whole place haunted by the demons that Balinese cosmology attributes to the sea (the opposite axis to their holy of holies, the inland volcano Gunung Agung). It served as first a leper colony and later, in the 17th and 18th centuries, as a slave port, but fortunes started to turn in 1839, when Danish merchant Mads Lange set Kuta up as a flourishing trading post, garnering him enough influence that he was able to get the Dutch to leave South Bali in peace when they first conquered the northern regencies in 1849. The emphasis turned from commerce to tourism in 1936, when US couple Bob

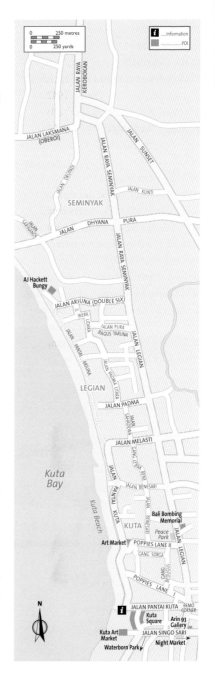

and Louise Koke set up the first independent hotel in Bali right on Kuta beach, entertaining a steady flow of Westerners until World War II arrived and the Japanese invaded in 1942. Tourism got going again in the 1960s and flourished in the 1980s and 1990s, only to be dealt a stunning blow with the October 2002 bombings (*see pp14–15*) that killed 202 people, decimating the local tourist trade overnight. But Kuta's vitality couldn't be extinguished, and these days it's once again the liveliest tourist centre in Bali.

Orientation

Formerly three separate villages, Kuta, Legian and Seminyak have grown into an amorphous conurbation thanks to the demands of tourism, hugging the western coast of South Bali in a compact rectangular shape. There are technically no hard and fast boundaries, but the accepted convention has Kuta running north from the Art Market up to Jalan Melasti; Legian, from Melasti north to Jalan Arjuna (aka Jalan Double Six); and Seminyak, from Arjuna north to Jalan Laksmana (aka Jalan Oberoi). The main road, Jalan Legian, stretches 6km (4 miles) through the three districts, turning into Jalan Raya Seminyak at the top end.

Most of the hotels, shops, restaurants and bars are on or between Jalan Legian to the east and the beach road to the west, Jalan Pantai Kuta (which turns into Jalan Pantai Arjuna), as well as on the *gangs* ('lanes') and roads that run between them, especially on Gang Poppies I and Gang Poppies II. For

Surfboards for hire on Kuta beach

road vehicles, the narrow streets are made even more difficult to navigate by means of a complicated 'one-way' system that the government has instituted. The areas just south of Kuta and just north of Seminyak are known, respectively, as Tuban and Petitenget.

Kuta

As Kuta is mainly a commercial area, there are few 'sights' to be found beyond the hundreds of restaurants, bars and shops. The walk (*see pp40–1*) gives a more detailed overview of the main things to see, but there are also plenty of small lanes and alleys in between Jalan Legian and Jalan Pantai Kuta that are good for a wander. Otherwise, just head west and hit the beach; it's the perfect spot for strolling at the water's edge, sunbathing or getting your hair plaited by the local hawkers. Strong currents make it better for surfing than swimming, so if you take a dip be sure to stay between the red and yellow flags.

Batik classes

Javanese artist Heru Purnomo is a master of *batik*, the Indonesian art of painting and dyeing cloth in beautiful designs using wax to form patterns. At his gallery a few blocks south of Bemo Corner, he offers three-day workshops (all materials included) that will let you take home your own *batik* masterpieces.
Arin Gallery. Jl Singo Sari 20, Gang Kresek 5, Kuta. Tel: (0361) 765 087. Workshop tuition: Rp500,000 (three days). Booking required.

Lifeguards keeping watch on Legian's beach

Night market

If you're up for a bit of culinary adventure, hit the *pasar senggol* (night market) at the southeastern edge of Kuta, where you can get large, cheap portions of local cuisine cooked up fresh and on the spot.

Jl Blambangan. Open: nightly.

Waterbom Park

This aquatic theme park in Tuban, only a few hundred metres south of Kuta Square, has pools, water slides, an inner-tube 'river', a climbing wall and a special playground for kids.

Jl Dewi Sartika (aka Jl Kartika), Tuban. Tel: (0361) 755 676.
www.waterbom.com. Open: 9am–6pm. Admission charge.

A tropical sunset in Kuta

Legian

A little more upmarket than Kuta, Legian has just as many shops, restaurants and bars, but with fewer young backpackers and more couples or families on holiday; it has a quieter, less rowdy feel that's evident as soon as you cross Jalan Melasti. The clothing boutiques are more stylish and nightlife more sophisticated, especially in the restaurants, lounges and clubs along the beach road, Jalan Pantai Arjuna (aka Jalan Blue Ocean Beach). The beach is also less crowded – but naturally has the same surf and sunsets as Kuta – so head north to Legian if you're looking for something a bit more sedate.

Seminyak

Seminyak, probably the most self-consciously hip area in Bali, is near enough to the action of Kuta and Legian but far enough away from the tourist throngs to make it popular with much of the island's expat community and many return holidaymakers who rent short- or long-term villas in the area. Even more upscale and subdued than Legian, it has a few exclusive hotels at the northern end (bordering the area known as Petitenget) and a host of trendy lounges and fashionable restaurants along Jalan Dhyana Pura and Jalan Laksmana, as well as some very stylish, very chic home-furnishing stores along Jalan Raya Seminyak.

Walk: Kuta's beach and town

Tourist-haven Kuta is generally the first destination in Bali for most visitors, and quite possibly the most commercial. This short walk is a good way to get acquainted with Kuta's beach and main shopping streets on your first day in town.

Approximately 2km (1¼ miles). Allow 1 hour.

Begin at Bemo Corner at the southern end of Jl Legian.

1 Jalan Legian

The small roundabout at the bottom of Jalan Legian is known as Bemo Corner, and even though it's not a corner and no *bemos* actually stop there, it's a popular landmark. Walking north along Kuta's main commercial street, Jalan Legian, will take you past all kinds of craft and souvenir shops, restaurants, bars, clothing stores and more.

Continue north to the Bali Bombing Memorial.

2 Bali Bombing Memorial

The ornately carved marble memorial in this plaza lists by name the 202 victims of the terrorist bombs that went off on this site in 2002 (*see pp14–15*). Across the street is Peace Park, a small grassy area where the Sari Club stood; its fence serves as an outdoor gallery for artwork or photographs.

Double back to the corner of Poppies Lane II and turn right.

3 Poppies Lane II

Walk west down 'Poppies 2', past more shops, bars and restaurants, and follow the road when it curves to the left and then to the right again. You'll pass a row of shops selling handicrafts, sarongs, bags and the like, ending up at Kuta's famous beach.

Turn left and walk south, either down Jl Pantai Kuta or on the beach itself.

4 Kuta beach

The origins of the Bali we know today started here in the 1930s, when the Kokes opened their small hotel on sleepy Kuta beach, at the southern end of Jalan Pantai Kuta. These days the beach is populated with tourists, surfboard rentals, hair plaiters, sarong and jewellery hawkers and cold drink vendors, but the beguiling combination of sand, sun and sea is no less lovely for it.

Continue down the beach or road and follow Jl Pantai Kuta when it turns to the right. Walk east about 50m (55 yds) and Kuta Square will be on your right.

5 Kuta Square

The shopping strip of Kuta Square is chock-a-block with cafés and shops for international brands of clothing, shoes and accessories. For an air-conditioned, haggle-free shopping experience, head to the multi-floor Matahari Department Store (halfway down on the left), which offers a massive supermarket, English-language bookshop, clothes, shoes, sporting equipment, electronics, housewares, gifts and more.

Continue south through Kuta Square and bear left, walking around the corner to the art market on the right.

6 Kuta Art Market

Walk west through Kuta's main *pasar seni* (art market), where you can browse through, yes, even more crafts stalls, and end up back at Kuta beach.

To get back to Bemo Corner, walk north up the beach and turn right onto Jl Pantai Kuta, and continue east for approximately 400m (440 yds).

Walk: Kuta's beach and town

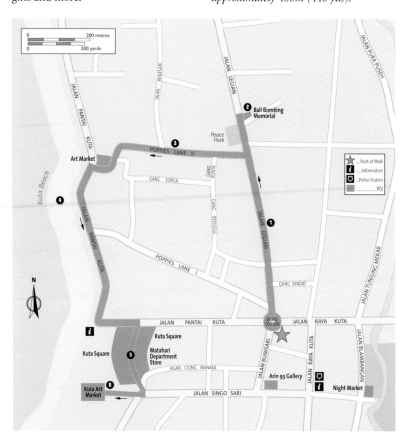

Bali's beaches

Despite its reputation as an island paradise, Bali's volcanic origins mean the coasts lack the glamour of pure white beaches and sparkling blue-green waters so often found in other tropical resorts. The tourist strongholds in the south see the most active sands and surf, while the remaining regions have mostly quiet fishing beaches that are best known for offshore diving and snorkelling.

South Bali

The first beach that most visitors hit, the long stretch of sand at **Kuta**, **Legian** and **Seminyak**, is famous for consistent tubes for surfing. It's great for sunbathing or strolling, but the rips can be too strong for swimming, and it's full of hawkers. But don't miss it at night, when breathtaking tropical sunsets streak their way through the clouds and the

Kuta beach is the first stop for most visitors to Bali

beachside nightlife at Legian goes into high gear.

To the east of Denpasar, **Sanur** has peaceful water suitable for families (although at low tide it is too exposed for swimming) and many diving and water-sports companies. **Tanjung Benoa** also has great water sports, and the high-end hotels of **Nusa Dua** sit beside some of the nicest white-sand beaches in Bali.

The western tip of the Bukit peninsula has some world-famous surfing beaches, too rough for swimming but worth a view for their stunning cliffside coastlines, pristine sands and beguilingly blue waters: **Dreamland**, **Bingin**, **Impossibles**, **Balangan**, and the surf meccas of **Suluban**, **Padang Padang** and **Uluwatu**. Further north, **Jimbaran** is known for excellent seafood served up fresh at beachside *warung*.

East Bali
A cautionary tale of overdevelopment, **Candi Dasa**'s once-beautiful beach got washed away when its coral reefs were harvested for limestone during the tourism boom of the 1970s. Ugly concrete jetties now protect the few bits that remain, but there's a quiet little beach with safe swimming just west of town off the main road. A spectacular underwater canyon offshore has wall dives and all kinds of large fish (suitable for advanced divers only, due to strong currents and cold water). The nearby ferry port of **Padang Bai** has a fairly secluded white-sand beach at Blue Lagoon, good for snorkelling and reachable by a short hike east from the main beach.

The offshore islands of **Nusa Penida** and **Nusa Lembongan** have some lovely, quiet beaches for swimming and snorkelling, as well as excellent options for experienced surfers and divers.

The sleepy fishing villages of **Amed** have mostly black-sand beaches good for a bit of relaxation and snorkelling, as well as diving the coral-reef walls and shipwrecks off Bali's east coast.

North and west Bali
The long black-sand beaches of **Lovina** are quiet and low-key, much like the resort itself – you'll see more fishing boats than tourists. It's good for a stroll or to sit with a drink, but don't bother with the much-advertised dolphin-spotting trips, which consist of noisy motorboats chasing after the poor creatures in the early morning in hope of a viewing.

To the far west, you'll find some of Bali's finest snorkelling and scuba diving on the coral reefs off **Permuteran** and the tiny island of **Pulau Menjangan**.

NUSA DUA AND BUKIT BADUNG

A scrubby, limestone peninsula connected to the bottom of Bali by a narrow isthmus, Bukit Badung (Badung Hill) rises almost 200m (650ft) above the Indian Ocean, offering the dramatically craggy cliffs and turbulent surf that attract vista-lovers and surfers alike. The custom-developed luxury resorts in the east have shopping, dining and water sports, while the west offers the sacred temple Pura Luhur Uluwatu, perched high above Bali's best surfing beaches, and the seafood *warung* at Jimbaran Bay to the north of these.

Poolside at a Nusa Dua resort

Jimbaran

The long stretch of this crescent-shaped beach on the western side of the isthmus is a study in contrasts. At the

A luxury hotel room in Nusa Dua

southern end are exclusive, expensive luxury resorts in the Nusa Dua mould, while further north are Jimbaran's renowned beachfront *warung*, serving up some of the cheapest, best fish and seafood in Bali – prawns, lobster, squid, clams, red snapper, tuna and more – caught each day and grilled fresh to order. The beach is lovely any time of the day, suitable for sunbathing or swimming (the surf is calmer than Kuta's), but really comes alive in the evenings as the sunset melts over the horizon and the *warung* fill up with customers.

Nusa Dua

In the 1980s, the Indonesian government earmarked the white-sand beaches of Nusa Dua for the development of luxury resorts in an effort to lure upmarket tourists and keep the locals out. While the resorts do indeed offer splendid facilities and pampered service – and the lack of aggressive hawkers (banned at Nusa Dua) can certainly be a relief – this constructed paradise won't offer much to those seeking an authentic experience of Balinese culture. But if a few days of sumptuous splendour in a sunny setting are what you're after, Nusa Dua is the place to splurge.

Apart from the (many) hotel-based spas and water-sports activities, Nusa Dua's attractions consist primarily of the world-class course at the **Bali Golf & Country Club** and the central **Bali Collection** shopping centre, featuring fashion outlets, shops and restaurants (along with both a British Tavern *and* a Starbucks). A number of livelier, but still tourist-orientated, restaurants are on Jalan Pantai Mengiat just outside the South Gate; continue past them and turn right onto Jalan Srikandi in the small village of **Bualu** for cheaper, more authentic Balinese *warung*.

Pura Luhur Uluwatu

One of Bali's 'directional temples' (*see pp84–5*), Uluwatu sits on a cliff almost 100m (330ft) above the roiling surf, protecting the island from evil forces from the southwest. First constructed in the 10th century by a Javanese holy man who built some of Bali's earliest temples, it was further developed in the 16th century by the priest who also built Pura Tanah Lot (*see p68*). The temple itself is not especially prepossessing, but the clifftop vistas more than make up for it – especially at sunset – with the best views found down a side road to the left.

Also popular are the wild monkeys who live here, but keep your possessions

The clifftop temple of Pura Luhur Uluwatu

The Chinese temple at Tanjung Benoa

close – they've learned to swipe hats and eyeglasses to hold for ransom (while canny locals sell bags of peanuts).
Open: daylight hours. Admission by donation; sarong and sash hire.

Surfing beaches

Just north of the temple at Uluwatu are Bali's most exciting surfing beaches, which enjoy consistent breaks and left-handers year-round (but are best from April to October when they get southeast winds from offshore). These beaches have reefs and strong currents and are not for beginner surfers, nor are they suitable for swimming or sunbathing, and many are accessible only by steep stairs. Advanced surfers will find them enjoyably challenging, though, and spectators can revel in the beautiful scenery. Going south down the coast, the beaches are grouped as follows: Balangan and Dreamland; Bingin, Impossibles and Padang

Padang; and Suluban and Uluwatu. Look for access-road signs on the main road to Uluwatu; a small road toll or parking fee may sometimes apply.

Tanjung Benoa

This old fishing village, on a narrow finger of land just north of Nusa Dua, was largely overlooked during the area's original tourist developments. Although the arrival of a number of nice hotels and resorts in recent years has transformed it into something like Nusa Dua's mid-market cousin, it has managed to retain some actual Balinese atmosphere. There are a number of restaurants – both fine dining and cheap *warung* – along the main road Jalan Pratama. A stroll through the village at the north end reveals evidence of its multicultural past as a trading centre, including the **Chinese Temple** (*Jl Segara Ening*) where one of Bali's oldest Chinese communities still worships.

The beach is not particularly appealing and the water exceedingly calm, but the area has excellent water sports, and numerous companies on Jalan Pratama offer competitive prices on water-skiing, jet-skiing, parasailing, wakeboarding, dolphin viewings, snorkelling trips and fishing and diving expeditions.

SANUR

A major tourist destination on the coast to the east of Denpasar, Sanur can be described as the family-friendly version of Kuta. It has a long, white-sand beach, plenty of shopping and dining opportunities and a relaxed atmosphere. A fringe of coral reef offshore keeps the waters calm and safe for swimming.

Orientation

Sanur's shoreline runs for 5km (3 miles) from North Sanur down through the areas known as Sindhu, Batujimbar, Semawang and Blanjong. The main road, Jalan Danau Tamblingan, following the shoreline about 500m (550 yds) back from the

A woman prepares a refreshing drink by chopping open a coconut

Locals gather on Sanur beach in the late afternoon to relax, swim and snack

beach, has a shady esplanade for strolling. Jalan Danau Tamblingan turns into Jalan Danau Toba in North Sanur.

Beach

Sanur's best attraction is the 5km (3 miles) of sandy beach stretching north to south along the town. Unlike in Kuta, there is no busy road right behind the beach, and as a result it is a much nicer place for relaxing and wandering around. A shaded footpath stretches the full length, connecting the hotels, restaurants and two small art markets that back right up onto the beach. Trees and *bale* platforms provide shade in the hottest hours. It's wise to stick to the hotel pool at low tide, as the sea gets too shallow for swimming, and

venturing far out can be dangerous due to currents. At any time, it's possible to engage one of the ladies hawking the beach for a relaxing massage under a tree. In the evening, locals come out on the beach to enjoy the evening breeze, and hawkers set up food stalls. All possible kinds of water sports can be practised along the beach, with several companies doing snorkelling, diving and fishing trips and offering activities such as windsurfing, jet-skiing and parasailing. Snorkelling and diving are not great at Sanur, so these trips usually involve a boat ride first.

Dance shows

Sanur is a good place to catch one of the *kecak* or *barong* dance shows. Look for announcements at the various hotels and restaurants in town to see a show while you dine, or go to one of the dance stages which host regular performances. Local travel agents run trips to the various dance stages, the most popular of which is 3km (2 miles) west of Sanur near Denpasar.

Museum Le Mayeur

Sanur attracted many foreign artists early last century. The Museum Le Mayeur is the house at the northern end of the beach where Belgian artist Adrien Jean Le Mayeur de Merpes (1880–1958) lived and worked. Le Mayeur arrived on Bali in 1932 and enjoyed painting scenes with Balinese women at work. He went on to marry one of his models, the beautiful local 15-year-old dancer Ni Polok, who features in many of the paintings on display. Ni Polok lived in the house until her death in 1985, after which the museum was founded. The pretty Balinese-style house, with its courtyards and gardens overlooking the beach, is arguably more interesting than the paintings themselves, but the museum is well worth a visit nevertheless.
Jl Hang Tuah. Open: Sun–Thur 8am–3pm, Fri 8am–1pm. Admission charge.

Orchid Garden

Due to the various microclimates at different altitudes, Bali has an incredible range of flora, and the

An eye to ward off evil spirits stares from a fishing boat on Sanur beach

variety of orchids that grow well in the fertile volcanic soil is amazing. This garden, a few kilometres north of Sanur along the road to Ubud, has thousands of them packed together, including the spectacular Bulbophylum species. You can take a guided tour of the gardens or walk around alone. The shop sells bulbs and plants, with export papers, as well as books and other souvenirs.

Jl Bypass Tohpati. Tel: (0361) 466 010.
www.baliorchidgardens.com.
Open: 8am–6pm.
Admission charge.

A pebble path leads to a villa room in a Sanur hotel

A spot of welcome shade on Sanur beach

Shopping

Jalan Danau Tamblingan, the road running parallel to the beach, is a pleasant street for strolling and shopping, even though the selection of souvenirs, crafts and clothes is not as varied as in Kuta. Special things to look for include *batik* clothes, paintings, carved wooden objects, baskets and sarongs. Good-value souvenirs can be found after haggling the price down at one of several art markets along the beach. For cheap and tasty Indonesian fare after dark, head to the night market at the corner of Jalan Danau Tamblingan and Jalan Sindhu.

THE RETURN OF TURTLE ISLAND

Just south of Sanur, Serangan (Turtle) Island was a popular snorkelling destination and a turtle breeding ground until it was selected for a hotel development. This never got beyond the preparation phase, by which time the island's beaches and reefs were all but destroyed. The turtles were already in danger from the locals, who captured the animals by the thousands; turtle meat is used for some Hindu rituals on Bali and the shells are turned into souvenirs. However, a new Turtle Conservation and Education Centre, co-funded by the Worldwide Fund for Nature, is a fresh start for the island. The centre aims to help bring back turtles in large numbers, educate locals about the animals and put an end to the illegal poaching.

Life cycles and rituals

The Balinese are a devout people whose unique brand of Hinduism, imported from India almost 2,000 years ago, is combined with ancient local animist beliefs. Family and community rituals are followed assiduously for all Balinese, starting from before birth and continuing through death. Some ceremonies are elaborate and costly affairs that require food, entertainment, and special clothing and supplies, so families sometimes delay until enough money can be saved, or hold shared ceremonies with others from their community.

Infancy

A few months before birth, a ceremony is held to pray for the baby's health. After delivery, the placenta and birthing fluids are buried near the front gate of the parents' house to keep the baby's soul tied to home. Parents and child are considered *sebel* (unclean) and cannot enter temples. At 12 days, a ceremony is held to learn which ancestor has been reincarnated, and after 42 days, the child is named and the *sebel* period ends. The baby is not allowed to touch the earth until 105 days have passed, at which point another ceremony is held to foretell its future life-path.

Childhood

The child's first birthday is celebrated after 210 days, or one year in the traditional Balinese calendar, and the little one is welcomed into the community with feasting and a ritual haircut. Another ceremony is held when the child's baby teeth fall out, with prayers offered for strong adult

Priests bless the crowd at a ceremony at Pura Goa Lawah

teeth. After puberty, the important tooth-filing ritual is held, as the Balinese believe that filing the six upper teeth into a straight line will diminish the negative influences of the six cardinal sins: jealousy, anger, greed, passion, intoxication and ignorance.

Marriage

All Balinese are expected to marry. The traditional way involves a formal request from the boy's family accompanied by expensive gifts and offerings. To save money (and heighten the sense of romance), many instead choose elopement. The boy and girl run off 'secretly', with her family (who no doubt helped her pack) pretending to be outraged and undertaking a supposedly thorough search. After a few days, the couple reappear and declare their love, and a formal ceremony is held, laden with sexual symbolism to ensure a fruitful marriage.

Death

Cremation is the most expensive and elaborate ceremony held, often taking so long to save up and prepare for, that the body is buried 'temporarily' (sometimes up to several years). A wooden sarcophagus is built to house the body along with a colourful cremation tower for carrying it. The

Ornate towers are built for cremation ceremonies

tower is spun around in circles to confuse the soul so it can't wander home to haunt its family. A joyful, musical ceremony is held, celebrating the release of the soul for reincarnation, and the sarcophagus is anointed with holy water and set alight. The ashes are then placed in a coconut and cast into a river or the sea. Three days later the family attends a purification ritual and, after 12 days, travels to one of the nine directional temples (see pp84–5) for a final ceremony with offerings to the gods for the soul's deification.

Central Bali

There's more to Bali than beaches, of course. The island has all kinds of natural beauty to be found in the interior: craggy mountains and brooding volcanoes, lush rainforests and bounding waterfalls, and rice fields flowing placidly down terraced hillsides. Besides the landscape, Central Bali also has one of the island's top destinations, Ubud, the undisputed hub of Balinese culture and home to the greatest concentration of art museums, dance and music troupes and crafts producers on the island.

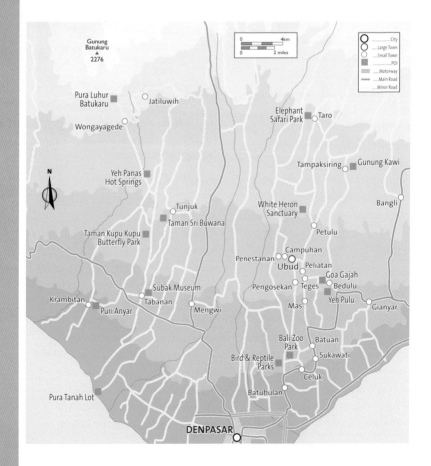

Many people dip into Central Bali on day trips from the south, which is understandable for those short on time. But anyone who wants to get a sense of the 'real' Bali would do well to leave the beach resorts and head inland, where Balinese culture can be found in its most vivid expression.

Orientation

Ubud is about 14km (9 miles) north of Denpasar, reachable by driving to Batubulan and on through the other villages of Bali's 'craft corridor'. Most of the main roads and the *bemo* routes follow the north-south orientation of the mountain ridges and river valleys, so east-west travel along the side roads is easier with private transport. Ubud has direct routes on to eastern Bali (through Gianyar) and Gunung Batur (through Tampaksiring), while the main road to Singaraja and the

THE WALLACE LINE

In 1859, the naturalist Alfred Russell Wallace noticed a remarkable difference between the fauna on Bali and that on Lombok, despite being only 35km (22 miles) apart. Similar animals could be found all along the Indonesian islands between Malaysia and Bali, but Lombok's species were common only to those stretching east, causing Wallace to theorise that low sea levels had once allowed free migration to either side but for some reason had been halted at his eponymous line. In the 20th century, plate tectonics research confirmed that the Lombok Strait sits on the edge of a continental shelf, with a massive underwater trench over 1,300m (4,265ft) deep in some places.

northwest is accessible from Mengwi, about 16km (10 miles) to the southwest. Tabanan is approximately 8km (5 miles) west of Mengwi and has a direct route to Pura Tanah Lot, but the north-south roads make a day trip here easier from South Bali than from Ubud.

The Ubud region is known for its high-quality arts and crafts

DENPASAR TO UBUD

The route from the southern areas to Ubud has wildlife attractions for young visitors and shopping and craft specialities for older ones.

Bali Bird Park and Bali Reptile Park

Impressively landscaped gardens serve as a backdrop for 250 species of exotic birds, including the endangered Bali starling. Next door are reptiles such as crocodiles, snakes – including an 8m (26ft) reticulated python – and Komodo dragons. Combination tickets are available.

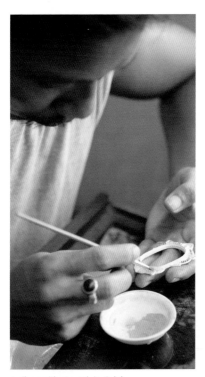

A silversmith at work in Celuk

Jl Serma Cok Ngurah Gambir, Singapadu. Tel: (0361) 299 352. Open: 9am–5pm. Admission charge.

Bali Zoo Park

Kids will also enjoy the Bali Zoo, just up the road from the bird and reptile parks, which features cassowaries, tigers, deer, camels, lions and other animals.
Jl Raya Singapadu, Singapadu. Tel: (0361) 294 356. Open: 9am–6pm. Admission charge.

Craft villages

The 13km (8-mile) stretch between Denpasar and Ubud is famous for villages that produce high-quality arts and crafts at roadside workshops. **Batubulan** has stone carvings of every size, with mythological figures like gods and demons, and animals, people and even abstract designs. **Celuk** is Bali's production centre for silver jewellery, which you can buy directly from the silversmiths or order custom-made. **Sukawati** has a *pasar seni* (art market) for local crafts and workshops for *wayang kulit* shadow puppets. **Batuan** was the origin of an eponymous school of painting (*see pp62–3*), but the art galleries and studios here feature a variety of styles. **Mas** has skilled woodcarvers working in hibiscus, mahogany, coconut and many other woods, making everything from *barong* masks and pocket-sized Buddhas to expert renditions of animals, people, and demons a metre or so tall.

UBUD

Nestled between rice paddies, river valleys and hilly ridges is Ubud, the cultural heart of Bali. What it lacks in beaches it makes up for with an unending array of dance and music performances, art museums and galleries, craft shops, pleasant hotels and spas and excellent restaurants. Despite the unavoidable commercialism, Ubud's vibrant culture exudes a more 'authentic' feel than the touristy spots down south, and many visitors prefer to base themselves here, especially as its central location is convenient for day trips around the island.

History

The local kingdom of Gianyar was founded in the early 1700s by the

Schoolgirls sharing secrets high above Ubud's river

cultured Sukawati family, who avidly supported performers and artisans at their court. At the end of the 19th century, Ubud was established as a minor court by a Sukawati prince, but when Gianyar became a Dutch protectorate in 1900, he was forced to concede as well. The new peace allowed Ubud to further develop artistic pursuits, attracting a host of intellectual and artistic expatriates in the 1930s – such as painters Walter Spies, Rudolf Bonnet and Theo Meier, musicologist Colin McPhee and anthropologist Margaret Mead – whose foreign connections helped raise Ubud's status as a cultural centre.

Orientation

Ubud's high street, Jalan Raya Ubud, runs east-west through town, with north-south streets crossing it. The centre of town – where you'll find the palace, main temple, market and tourist office – is at the intersection of Jalan Raya Ubud and Jalan Monkey Forest.

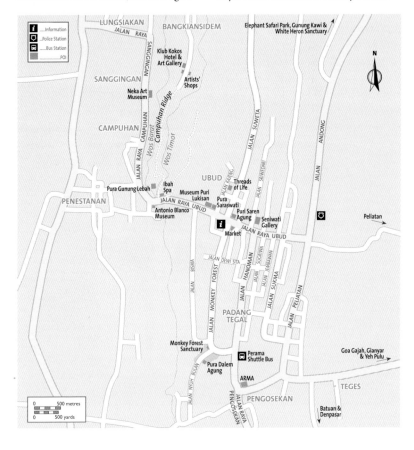

The Ubud area has grown to encompass the villages immediately adjacent, including Campuhan, Padang Tegal, Peliatan, Pengosekan and Penestanan. Walking south down Jalan Hanoman will take you through Padang Tegal to Pengosekan, walking west on Jalan Raya Ubud leads to Penestanan, Campuhan and Sanggingan via a bridge over the river Wos, and Peliatan can be found by walking east on Jalan Raya Ubud and turning right at the main T-junction.

Agung Rai Museum of Art (ARMA)

ARMA's sizeable and rewarding collection presents numerous styles of art by Balinese, Indonesian and foreign artists; Walter Spies' eerie 1930 *Calonarang* is the only work of his exhibited anywhere on Bali. Also a gallery and cultural centre, the ARMA has an open-air stage for dance performances, a library and research centre and a host of practical workshops in Balinese fine and performing arts, crafts, history and cookery.
Jl Raya Pengosekan, Pengosekan. Tel: (0361) 975 742. www.armamuseum.com. Open: 9am–6pm. Admission charge.

Antonio Blanco Museum

You can't miss the entrance to the former house of the eccentric and campy Spanish painter who settled here in the early 1950s. The self-styled 'Dalí

Entrance to the Antonio Blanco Museum, Campuhan

of Bali', Blanco painted mostly portraits of beautiful young Balinese women in various states of undress, including his *legong* dancer wife. A flamboyantly designed museum houses his works (including a closed-door exhibit of erotica), and there's also a tropical aviary, a gallery of other works and Blanco's studio.
Jl Raya Campuhan, Campuhan. Tel: (0361) 975 502. www.blancobali.com. Open: 9am–5pm. Admission charge.

Monkey Forest Sanctuary and Pura Dalem Agung

One of Ubud's most popular attractions is this small forest at its southern end, home to three temples and a hundred or so long-tailed grey macaques. They're photogenic but definitely not tame, and have learned to steal hats and eyeglasses from passing tourists to extort handouts of food in exchange. The temperamental creatures have been known to bite if provoked, so it's best to keep your distance, and never try to pet or hand-feed them. Inside the forest is Ubud's striking 'Great Temple of the Dead', with fierce carvings of the widow-witch Rangda devouring children.

Jl Monkey Forest. Tel: (0361) 971 304. Open: 8am–6pm. Admission charge; donation for sarong and sash hire (temple).

Entrance to the sacred monkey forest in Ubud

Museum Puri Lukisan

The first major art museum in Ubud, Puri Lukisan (Palace of Paintings) was opened in 1956 by Agung Sukawati and Rudolf Bonnet (*see pp62–3*) in an attempt to keep Balinese works from disappearing overseas. Although its collection contains a large number of Pita Maha pieces in a setting of lovely gardens and pavilions, a visit to the larger Neka Museum offers a far better overview of Balinese art. Still, it's a worthwhile supplement for devoted Balinese art fans.

Jl Raya Ubud. Tel: (0361) 975 136. www.mpl-ubud.com. Open: 9am–5pm. Admission charge.

Neka Art Museum

With over 400 works of traditional and contemporary Balinese painting, this is the largest and most comprehensive art museum on the island, with six separate pavilions dedicated to all styles of Balinese painting, individual artists such as I Gusti Nyoman Lempad, contemporary Indonesian art, expatriate artists like Rudolf Bonnet (Dutch) and Donald Friend (Australian), and a collection of 1930s photographs of Balinese life taken by the US founder of the first hotel in Kuta (*see pp36–7*). Artworks are for sale at the museum's gallery on Ubud's main road.

Jl Raya Sanggingan, Sanggingan. Tel: (0361) 975 074. www.museumneka.com. Open: 9am–5pm. Admission charge.

Ubud has numerous craft shops along its streets

Pura Saraswati

This water palace designed by local genius I Gusti Nyoman Lempad has a temple to the Hindu goddess of learning set among gardens and a huge lotus pond. A restaurant at the southern end, Cafe Lotus, offers a beautiful view and front-row seats for the dance performances held here.
Jl Raya Ubud. Open: daily.
Free admission.

Puri Saren Agung (Ubud Palace)

The Sukawati family palace makes a beautiful setting for nightly dance performances, and also offers guestrooms to the public (*see p164*).

Visitors are welcome to stroll through the grounds for free.
Jl Raya Ubud, Ubud.

Seniwati Gallery of Art by Women

Balinese women feature prominently as subjects for much of Balinese art, but the local museums have a dearth of paintings by female artists. The Seniwati Gallery was founded in 1991 by a British expat in order to display and sell works by female Balinese painters. It also runs a non-profit girls' school (the only one in the area) that teaches artistic skills.
Jl Sriwedari 2, Ubud. Tel: (0361) 975 485. www.seniwatigallery.com.
Open: Tue–Sun 9am–5pm.
Free admission.

Balinese dances are performed nightly in Ubud

Balinese painting

As in other cultures, Balinese art was first practised by anonymous, unpaid artists producing commissioned works for palaces and temples. With the downfall of Balinese kings after the Dutch occupation, native art began a precipitous decline until the Dutch implemented their 'Ethical Policy' (*see pp100–1*) in an attempt to preserve and develop the indigenous culture.

Soon the Dutch-promoted tourism trade of the 1930s brought over affluent Europeans and Americans

The classical *wayang* or Kamasan style depicts stories from Hindu epics

who quickly developed a passion for Balinese art. This created a brand-new market for Balinese artists, who began to experiment with new themes and different styles, and could now take credit (and get paid) for their works. A number of expatriate artists from Europe, such as Walter Spies (German) and Rudolf Bonnet (Dutch), started relocating to Bali, becoming involved with communities of local artists and introducing Western techniques and styles (although in some cases the extent of their influence has been overstated).

But there was a downside to the booming tourist market: increased demand caused artists to concentrate on quantity over quality, and inferior imitations started appearing. In 1936, the (titular) prince of Ubud, Cokorda Gede Agung Sukawati, and renowned local artist I Gusti Nyoman Lempad recruited Spies and Bonnet to help found the Pita Maha ('Great Vitality') movement, with the mission of encouraging artists to move away from mass-market work and instead develop their talent and artistic expressions. The movement ended only a few years later with World War II and the death of Walter Spies;

much of the works it produced later became the basis for the collection at Ubud's Museum Puri Lukisan. After World War II and the fight for Indonesian independence had ended, Balinese art began to redevelop itself, and renewed tourism and a new generation of expat artists brought fresh markets and influences into the mix. Today, Balinese art thrives in Ubud, which has the greatest concentration of museums, galleries and studios on the island.

Painting styles

Although there are transitional and hybrid examples that resist easy definition, Balinese art is generally divided into six schools (most named after their place of origin):

The 20th-century Pengosekan style focuses on animals and nature

- *Wayang* (puppet) or **Kamasan** – the classic, Javanese-influenced style, featuring flattened figures from Hindu epics in three quarter profile, limited colours, religious themes and large canvases filled with multitudes of characters.
- **Ubud** – developed in the 1930s, with the use of realistic techniques such as perspective, shadow and proportion, portraying secular subjects relating to ordinary Balinese life.
- **Batuan** – also 1930s, similar to *wayang* in the level of detail and activity, but with darker, more

modern and introspective themes and social commentaries, typically using a black-ink wash.
- **Pengosekan** – a 1960s style focusing on depictions of animals and nature, usually birds and flowers, often in pastel colours.
- **Young Artists** – also 1960s, developed by Dutch painter Arie Smits and his young students in Penestanan, featuring colourful, expressionistic and detailed depictions of daily life.
- **Academic** – referring to recent generations of academy-trained Balinese and other Indonesian artists, working in more modern, Western-influenced and abstract styles.

AROUND UBUD
To the east
Goa Gajah (Elephant Cave)

This site dates back to the 11th century and is thought to have operated as both a temple and a spiritual retreat for Hindu priests. The gender-separated bathing pools outside the cave were used for ritual cleansing before prayer. The cave façade has a mass of enthusiastic, almost abstract carvings, with the entrance doubling as the gaping mouth of a *boma*, the protective spirits found above temple doorways and meant to frighten off evil spirits. Inside, niches in the cave walls were used for meditation by the priests. A statue of Men Brayut with her many children (*see box, p92*) stands outside

The Elephant Cave at Goa Gajah

the cave. The guides here can be rather insistent, so negotiate their fee in advance if you want to use one.
Jl Raya Goa Gajah, past Teges.
Open: 9am–5pm. Admission charge and guide fee.

Yeh Pulu

A few hundred metres east of Goa Gajah, down a long hillside path in a tiny hamlet, are the carved panels at Yeh Pulu, thought to date back to the 14th century. Stretching 25m (82ft) across a single section of rock wall, they show several different scenes of Balinese people, including princesses, priests and boar hunters, along with carvings of Hindu deities like Ganesha, the elephant god. Unlike Goa Gajah, quiet Yeh Pulu gets few tourists, so it may be just you and the temple guardian, a delightful old woman who will bless you with water from the holy spring for an extra donation. Yeh Pulu is also accessible by a lovely guided walk through the rice paddies from Goa Gajah.
Tengah, near Bedulu. Open: daylight hours. Admission by donation.

To the north
Elephant Safari Park

Elephants rescued from the logging industry in Sumatra now reside at this wildlife park, where you can hand-feed and pet them or even take an elephant ride for an extra fee. There's an elephant museum, a large restaurant and, of course, a gift shop. Bali

Adventure Tours (*see p166*) own the park and a visit is included in some of their tour packages.

Taro. Tel: (0361) 721 480. Open: 9am–5pm. Admission charge.

Gunung Kawi

Down in the Pakerisan river valley are these amazing 11th-century *candi* ('shrines'), hewn directly into the cliffs. Set in two separate groups, they're thought to be royal memorials to King Anak Wungsu and his wives and consorts. A group of adjacent rock-cut rooms are thought to be former monks' cells, and you can opt for a guided walk through the rice paddies to the tenth *candi*, possibly built for a high-court minister.

Tampaksiring. Open: 8am–6pm. Admission charge and guide fee.

Petulu White Heron Sanctuary

These thousands of white herons and cattle egrets are believed by locals to contain the souls of the 100,000 Balinese massacred in Indonesia's political purges of 1965; many of the victims were buried nearby and the birds mysteriously appeared soon afterwards. Every morning at sunrise over 20,000 birds fly off for food, blanketing the trees like a snowstorm upon their return at sunset (around 6pm).

Petulu, approximately 3km (2 miles) north of Ubud on Jl Andong. Admission by donation.

The carved rockface at Gunung Kawi

Walk: Ubud's backroads

This route through the countryside around Ubud can be combined with trips to the Neka or Antonio Blanco museums (see pp59, 60). Be sure to bring water and plenty of sun protection as there are long stretches with no shade; it's wise to start early in the morning or wait until the afternoon to avoid the hottest parts of the day. The walk can also be done in the reverse order, starting from the Ibah Spa & Luxury Villas on Jl Raya Ubud and ending up on Jl Raya Sanggingan, where you can catch a bemo *to the museums or to Ubud.*

Approximately 7km (4 miles). Allow 2–5 hours, depending on meals and museum visits.

Start by taking a *bemo* to the Neka Art Museum for a visit and then walking north from there (roughly 20 minutes), or take the *bemo* directly to Lungsiakan's main road where it meets Jalan Raya Sanggingan. Walk north through the villages of Lungsiakan and Payogan.

1 Lungsiakan and Payogan

These villages will give you an idea of typical Balinese country life. You'll see local temples, the *banjar* (village council), family compounds and village residents going about their day.

Continue along the road as it bears east, down to the river gorge. Cross the bridge and follow the road as it climbs up again and offers picturesque valley views. When you eventually come to a T-junction, turn right and walk south through the village of Bangkiansidem.

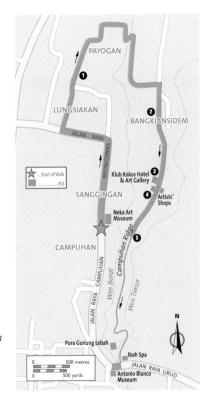

The rice paddies of Bangkiansidem

2 Bangkiansidem

This small village has a number of terraced rice paddies on either side of the road, where you may see farmers tending their rice plants.

Continue walking south to Klub Kokos on your right.

3 Klub Kokos hotel and art gallery

This hotel (*see p164*) has an airy café where you can stop and get a cool drink or a light meal, as well as a public art gallery filled with works from local artists.

Continue walking south to some artists' shops further down the road.

4 Artists' shops

Have a browse through the intricate paintings; the artists will happily explain the methods they use to produce their works. If you were thinking of bringing a Balinese artwork home, buying one here can save money and ensure the direct support of local artisans.

Continue walking south until the road turns into a path with paving stones. Follow it south along the ridge.

5 Campuhan ridge

This path lines the ridge between the Wos Barat and Wos Timor rivers, and is surrounded by the tall, sharp elephant grass used for thatched roofs. To your right you'll see the buildings of Campuhan (including the Neka Art Museum), and on the left, the countryside north of Ubud.

Continue south until you get to the Pura Gunung Lebah temple. Cross over the bridge and walk up the hill to the driveway of the Ibah Spa & Luxury Villas; turn right and walk down to Jl Raya Ubud. A left turn will take you back to Ubud, or turn right and cross back over the river to visit the Antonio Blanco Museum, just past the bridge.

The river ridge path, Campuhan

Walk: Ubud's backroads

AROUND TABANAN

'The rice basket' of Bali, green and fertile Tabanan has some of the most beautiful rice-paddy terraces on Bali (*see* Drive, *pp70–71*). Unlike his eastern counterparts, the king of Tabanan refused to collaborate with the Dutch. In 1906 they seized control of the region, but because he did not commit *puputan*, his descendants live on today at the Puri Anyar palace in Krambitan.

Pura Luhur Batukaru

Also known as the 'Garden Temple', this directional temple (*see pp84–5*) is set on the forested slopes of Gunung Batukaru, Bali's second-tallest mountain (2,276m/7,467ft) and its third holiest after Agung and Batur. Not many tourists visit, so you may find yourself wandering around the moss-covered monuments and *meru* towers with only the brightly coloured forest birds for company.

Wongayagede. Open: daylight hours. Donation for sarong and sash hire.

Pura Tanah Lot

One of Bali's most striking holy sites, this sea temple was built by the 16th-century Javanese priest Nirartha. It's set against crashing waves on a small, rocky islet a few metres offshore, accessible only at low tide (be prepared to do a bit of wading), but the headlands offer fantastic coastal views regardless. Only worshippers are allowed up to the temple, but for an extra donation you can receive a blessing with holy water and grains of rice from the priests at its base, or pet one of the sacred coral snakes that live in the cliff caves opposite. Sunsets at Tanah Lot are spectacular but crowded, so visit earlier in the day if you want to beat the rush; it's an easy and common day trip from the south.

Open: daylight hours. Admission charge.

Puri Anyar

You can visit this traditional palace or even stay the night (*see 'Directory' accommodation listing, p166*).

Subak Museum and Traditional Balinese House

This modest museum on the eastern end of Tabanan features exhibits and artefacts explaining Balinese rice farming and the complex irrigation

A wooden statue of Garuda at Puri Anyar, near Tabanan

system devised by the *subaks* ('rice-farmers' collectives') (*see pp72–3*).
Across from the museum is a model Traditional Balinese House showing the layout of a typical family compound. (The turn-off is well signed but the museum is not; look for the multi-storey building with the moat-like pond in front.)
Jl Raya Kediri, Tabanan. Tel: (0361) 810 315. Open: Mon–Thur & Sat 8am–4.30pm, Fri 8am–3pm. Closed: Sun. Admission charge.

Taman Kupu Kupu (Bali Butterfly Park)
The enclosed gardens of this park host a variety of butterfly species found all over Indonesia. It may not be worth a trip on its own, but if you're passing by it's a pleasant diversion.
Jl Batukaru, Wanasari. Tel: (0361) 814 282. Open: 8am–5pm. Admission charge.

Taman Sri Buwana Village Life Programme
This unique cultural programme offers hands-on experience in traditional Balinese farming methods, with a day tour through a small village's family compounds, elementary school and rice paddies, as well as home-cooked lunch at the village. Transport is included in the ticket price. Advanced booking required.
Tunjuk, near Tabanan.
Tel: (0361) 742 5929.
www.balivillagelife.com

Pura Tanah Lot, Bali's most photographed temple

Central Bali

Drive: Extraordinary Jatiluwih

This drive will take you through the fertile lands of the Tabanan region, 'the rice basket' of Bali, to the stunning rice paddies and magnificent views around the village of Jatiluwih ('Extraordinary'), located almost 800m (2,625ft) above sea level at the base of Gunung Batukaru, the second-highest mountain on Bali. The important temple of Pura Luhur Batukaru and some other sights can also be visited on the way, or skipped if short on time.

Instead of driving yourself, it's better to hire a local driver with a Jeep or 4WD so you can sit back and enjoy the views instead of worrying about the road. Also be aware that this area is cooler than the coast and gets more rain.

Approximately 50km (31 miles) round-trip. Allow 2–4 hours, depending on stops.

Begin on the main road in the town centre of Tabanan.

1 Tabanan

The former capital of an ancient kingdom that was one of the last holdouts against the Dutch in 1906, today Tabanan (*see pp68–9*) is the administrative capital for one of the country's most fertile regions.

From the main road, head north on Jl Gunung Agung to Wanasari, following the signs for Pura Luhur Batukaru.

2 Taman Kupu Kupu Butterfly Park

Approximately 8km (5 miles) north of Tabanan, in Wanasari, you'll see signs

for this butterfly park (*see p69*). It's worth a short visit if you're a particular

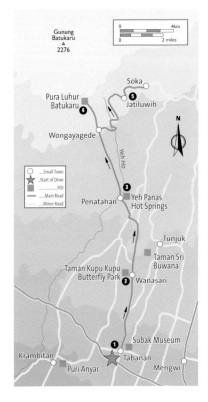

The extraordinary rice paddies of Jatiluwih

fan of the fluttering things or fancy a walk through some lovely gardens.
Continue north along the road to Penatahan.

3 Yeh Panas Hot Springs

A further 8km (5 miles) up the road in Penatahan is the Yeh Panas Hot Springs Resort (*Tel: (0361) 262 356*), which features a pool of sulphurous waters thought to be good for the skin. Non-guests can take a dip for a fee, or have lunch in the open-air restaurant overlooking the Yeh Ho river.
Continue north to the T-junction in Wongayagede. To visit Pura Luhur Batukaru, drive straight ahead another 2.5km (1¹/₂ miles). To go directly to Jatiluwih, turn right at the junction and continue on.

4 Pura Luhur Batukaru

The 'Garden Temple' is one of Bali's holiest sites (*see p68*), but with few tourists visiting, it's also one of the quietest, with a lush, serene forest setting that's home to a diverse number of local bird species.
From the temple, drive south 2.5km (1¹/₂ miles) back to the junction and turn left to head east towards Jatiluwih.

5 Jatiluwih

The winding roads on the ridges of Gunung Batukaru lead to some of the most beautiful terraced rice paddies in all of Bali, with amazing views right down to the southern coast in some places. If the day is clear you may even see mighty Gunung Agung to the east. There are a few restaurants along the way if you'd like a meal with a view, including one located on your left just before the village of Soka, where the views end.
Head back west along the same road, turning left at Wongayagede to return to Tabanan, or right to visit Pura Luhur Batukaru.

Offerings are made to Dewi Sri, the goddess of the rice, to ask for good harvests

Rice farming

Feeding much of the world's population every day, rice is one of the most cultivated plants anywhere and is of enormous importance to the local economies on Bali and Lombok. Essentially a grass that is very tolerant of water, rice – and its cultivation – has transformed the landscapes of Bali and Lombok over the centuries, and is even embedded in local religion.

Cultivation and preparation

Rice on Bali and Lombok is mainly cultivated on the alluvial plains to the south of the volcanoes on either island, as the monsoon rains mainly fall here. The man-made terraced ponds or rice paddies dotted all over the

A Sasak woman threshing rice in the traditional way

landscape guarantee ideal growing conditions for the plants; there's copious fertile soil and abundant water to feed the thirsty plants. Although rice does well on dry land too, the shallow layer of water they are planted in prevents weeds from gaining the upper hand over the young rice plants. Once the rice is taller, the water can then be drained. Rice cultivation is very labour-intensive, and dozens of people are involved in planting seeds at nurseries, preparing the paddy, planting the young shoots in the water, harvesting the rice and ploughing the paddy again. The hard work really starts after the harvest. The seeds have to be separated from the grass, and the husks then have to be removed from the grains by repeated threshing. Much of the work is still done by hand.

Irrigation and religion

Farmers regularly pray at the many shrines across Bali dedicated to Dewi Sri, the rice goddess, but for their water supply they need more help. Coordinated irrigation planning is essential if each rice paddy on the large alluvial plains is to get water. An incredibly complex system of ancient

The Balinese devised massive irrigation systems for their rice paddies

irrigation channels controlled by *subaks* (irrigation associations) distributes the water evenly over the fields. On Bali, farmers gather at so-called water temples to discuss watering schedules and when to plan fallow periods, an effective way to keep rice pests from returning, reducing the need for pesticides and also preventing exhaustion of the soil. Religion, agriculture and regional cooperation are combined in the *subak* system (*see also 'Subak Museum', pp68–9*). In the late 1960s, however, Indonesia's 'Green Revolution' brought new, high-yield rice varieties, chemical fertiliser and pesticide into play, which allowed farmers to harvest more crops in a year but lessened the significance of the water temples, and saw the poisoning of soil and surface water by pesticides become a problem. Many farmers have since chosen to return to the old methods.

Rice, nature and landscape

Though the local farmers on Bali and Lombok are mainly concerned with rice yields, nature and the tourism industry also benefit from the maintenance of the rice-paddy system. The wet fields are home to an incredible array of insects, frogs and the animals that eat them in turn. The tourism industry discovered the beauty of lush green rice paddies long ago, and some of the world's most luxurious hotels can now be found in and around Ubud, all boasting of their magnificent rice-paddy views, and trying to prevent any new development within sight.

East Bali

Once the base of Bali's most powerful rulers and a major centre for arts and culture, East Bali is today known more for quiet resorts, noteworthy dive spots and transport to offshore destinations, but most of all, for having some of the holiest temples, lakes and mountains in Bali, namely the mighty Gunung Agung (Great Mountain) and its 'Mother Temple' Besakih, as well as the fiery Gunung Batur with its eponymous crater lake and temple.

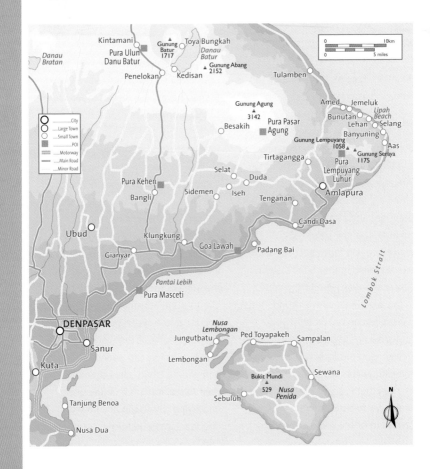

The enchanting pools at Tirtagangga Water Palace hint at past royal glories

History

The east was Bali's most politically fractious area, with numerous kingdoms fighting for power throughout its history. The Majapahit rulers from Java set up their main court at Samprangan (outside Gianyar), leading to a flowering of arts and culture that led to Bali's Golden Age under 16th-century King Batu Renggong of Gelgel. Other courts were located at Gianyar, Bangli, Klungkung and Karangsem (now called Amlapura), which in its day was the most powerful kingdom in Bali, with dominion over Lombok and parts of Sumbawa. The Dutch invasion led to more internecine squabbling, with rival kings selling each other out and surrendering to the Dutch for protection, until the last independent kingdom of Bangli capitulated in 1909.

Orientation

Most visitors come from the south (a new coastal bypass road is in the last stages of completion), basing themselves in Padang Bai or Candi Dasa and exploring the region with day trips. A main road from Singaraja cuts through the inland mountain area serving traffic from the north. The far east coast has the remote and still largely untouched Amed resort and the popular *Liberty* wreck dive site at Tulamben.

THE EAST COAST

Lying in the shadow of the holy volcano Gunung Agung, the east coast has a number of both cultural and natural attractions for visitors wanting to expand their itinerary past South Bali: ancient temples and palaces, unique diving sites, and subdued resort areas that offer the perfect little hideaway from the rest of the island (and the world). If you're planning any offshore trips, you can catch boats to Nusa Penida, Lombok and the Gili Islands at Padang Bai.

Amed

Consisting of a number of peaceful fishing villages, Amed is a haven far from the madding crowd (*see 'Getting away from it all', pp120–21*).

Candi Dasa

There's not much of a beach scene to be found at Candi Dasa (*see p43*), but this quiet little town is not without its charms. A number of lovely mid-range and upmarket hotels and restaurants stretch along a kilometre or so of Jalan Raya Candi Dasa, its main road. On its eastern end, a large, waterlily-filled

---

BALINESE GODS

The Balinese believe strongly in supernatural forces that require continual appeasement. All Hindu gods are manifestations of the supreme deity Sanghyang Widi Wasa, but the three highest are Brahma the Creator, married to Saraswati, the goddess of learning, Wisnu (Vishnu) the Preserver, who rides the half-man/half-bird Garuda (also the name of Indonesia's troubled airline), and Siwa (Shiva) the Destroyer, married to Durga, queen of the demons. Temple decorations denote these three by the colours red, black and white respectively. Lesser deities, originating in native animist beliefs, are worshipped as the goddesses of rice (Dewi Sri), lakes (Dewi Danu), and financial prosperity (Dewi Melanting), as well as the god of the sea (Dewa Baruna).

---

lagoon sits across from the village temple. If you're desperate for sand, there are pockets of nice beaches to be found in the areas past either end of the main road, but even at the hotels in the centre you can still relax on their waterfront terraces and enjoy a swimming pool and striking views of Nusa Penida and Nusa Lembongan just across the Badung Strait. As a tourist-centred but still quite sleepy resort (the nearest ATMs are in the nearby district capital Amlapura), it makes a better base for exploring East Bali than does Padang Bai, which mostly caters for harbour trade and hasn't as many nice options for dining and accommodation.

Padang Bai

Both the Perama tourist boat to the Gili Islands and the ferries to Nusa Penida and Lombok depart from the small harbour town of Padang Bai. Most people rush through, but there's ample reason to linger here for a day or two. Padang Bai's beach is lined with good accommodation and food options and is far enough from the ferry terminal to be clean and enjoyable. Follow the signs across the small headland and you'll quickly reach the aptly named Blue Lagoon Bay, a pretty cove with two *warung*. There's superb snorkelling and diving to be done here, with a great variety of fish. You can simply snorkel in the shallows or hire a boat to take you out to other good spots.

Pantai Lebih

Black-sand Lebih Beach has some good surfing but is extremely popular with locals for the dozens of seafood *warung* ranged along it and serving up the day's catch. Try the *sate languan* (grilled fish on skewers) or the *ikan pepes* (spiced fish steamed on the grill in banana leaf). Many of the eateries are open for lunch, but the scene is liveliest from early evening through to 11pm or midnight.

9km (5¹/₂ miles) south of Gianyar.

Pura Goa Lawah

A short distance west of Padang Bai is the temple at Goa Lawah (Bat Cave), one of Bali's 'directional temples' (*see pp84–5*), charged with protecting the islanders from evil forces emanating from the southeast. You won't find any caped superheroes here, though – just thousands of bats hanging from the walls of the cave mouth, as well as the accompanying smell. But as one of Bali's most important temples, ceremonies are held here on a regular basis, so there's a good chance of seeing one even if you decide just to turn up. The cave is alleged to run all the way to Besakih Temple on Gunung Agung, some 19km (12 miles) away, although since it's also reputed to be the home of the giant snake-deity Naga Basuki, you may want to stick to more conventional routes.

Guesthouses, fishing boats and jungle along Padang Bai's seafront

4km (2¹/₂ miles) west of Padang Bai.
Open: daylight hours. Admission charge.

Taman Gili

Located in the centre of the district
capital Klungkung, the fascinating
Taman Gili (Island Park) is all that
remains of the palace built in 1710 for
the then most powerful king on Bali.
Most of the once-glorious complex was
destroyed in the final battles with the
Dutch in 1908, but still standing are the
Kerta Gosa (Hall of Justice), where the
highest court cases were heard, the Bale
Kambung (Floating Pavilion), built in
the middle of an ornamental pool, a
giant *kulkul* ('wooden bell') tower and a
huge gateway. The ceilings of the Kerta
Gosa are covered in narrative paintings
in the classic Kamasan style (*see*
pp62–3), recounting tales from the
Mahabharata (*see box, p91*), while
those at the Bale Kambung depict

Balinese astrological symbols and Pan
and Men Brayut with their unruly
brood (*see box, p92*). There's also a
museum with photos and artefacts
from the former palace.
Jl Puputan, Klungkung. Open:
8am–5pm. Admission charge.

Tenganan

Just north of Candi Dasa is the small
Bali Aga ('Original Balinese') village of
Tenganan. The Bali Aga people rejected
the Javanese social and religious
reforms brought to Bali by the Hindu
rulers of the Majapahit kingdom in
1343, choosing instead to retain their
traditional social structures and
animist-based religion. Today the
village of Tenganan is known for being
the only place on Bali where a 'double-
ikat' form of cloth called *gringsing* is
woven (*see p17*). Each piece is done by
hand, a painstaking process that can

The cave at Pura Goa Lawah is home to thousands of bats

Tenganan is the only village on Bali where 'double *ikat*' cloth is made

take up to a year. Also available for purchase are woven baskets and traditional Balinese calligraphy inscribed onto *lontar* palms, usually as religious calendars or extracts from the great Hindu epic the *Ramayana* (*see box, p91*).

A donation is requested to visit Tenganan, and a guide will take you through the village to see its temple, village hall and very likely even his family compound. Tenganan is located 4km (2¹/₂ miles) up a side road just west of Candi Dasa; you can hire a car or else walk along Jalan Raya Candi Dasa and pay an *ojek* to take you up the hill to

Tenganan, and then enjoy a pleasant walk back.

THE NOSE KNOWS?

According to legend, the 14th-century ruler of eastern Bali lost one of his prized stallions, and when the villagers of Tenganan found its carcass, the king offered them a reward. The villagers asked to be given the land around the horse's body, extending to wherever its odor could still be smelled. The king sent a minister with a keen nose, who set off from Tenganan with the village chief, but no matter how far they walked, the stench was inescapable. The minister gave up and ceded the villagers their land – never knowing that the chief had been carrying with him a hidden piece of the dead horse's flesh.

Tirtagangga Royal Water Park

One of the most picturesque places in all of Bali, the Royal Water Park at Tirtagangga was built by the last king of Karangasem in 1948 as a hot-weather retreat. Pretty gardens surround various fountains and ornamental pools with colourful *koi* fish gliding past statues and stepping stones. There are two larger (and fish-free) pools available for swimming. The restaurant offers beautiful views down a terraced rice-paddy valley to the ocean. There is a small market in front with food kiosks, and the small Japanese restaurant just east of the park hangs right over the valley, offering the best views of all. *www.tirtagangga.com. Open: 8am–7pm. Admission charge and guide fee.*

The *candi bentar* gates and stairs of Pura Penataran Agung, Besakih

Tulamben

One of Bali's most popular dive sites is found here, the so-called USS *Liberty* wreck (the ship's real name was the USAT *Liberty Glo*). In early 1942, this military cargo ship was crippled by a Japanese torpedo in the Lombok Strait and towed to Tulamben beach so its inventory of railway parts and rubber could later be collected. The Japanese invaded Bali just weeks later, and the ship mouldered away on Tulamben's beach until 1963, when the eruption of Gunung Agung sent it crashing into the sea. It lies in several easily accessible pieces just 50m (164ft) directly offshore, covered in coral and hosting an abundance of marine life – not to mention the human kind. Due to its popularity, many divers come here on day trips and the wreck can get a bit crowded between 11am and 4pm. Most of the dive centres in the area also offer accommodation, so one option is to stay in Tulamben overnight and dive early to beat the crowds. Night dives, especially during the full moon, are also an unforgettable experience.

THE INLAND VOLCANOES

The most dominant natural forces on Bali – helpful and malevolent by turns – are the sacred volcanoes in the northeastern parts of the island. Their fearsome eruptions have led to death and devastation, and yet Balinese agriculture is utterly dependent on the rich, fertile volcanic soil and the large crater lakes that feed rivers and streams all over the island. A sunrise trek up to one of the lofty summits can be a defining experience for any visitor to Bali.

Besakih

The holiest, 'mother' temple of Bali, Besakih is actually a complex of almost 30 temples and shrines set 1,000m (3,280ft) up the eastern side of Gunung Agung, with the largest and most significant temple being Pura Penataran Agung. Use of the site for religious ceremonies dates back to at least the 8th century, with successive rounds of additions over the centuries until 1917, when it was decimated by an earthquake and had to be rebuilt all over again. Festivals and ceremonies are held here regularly; schedules are available at any tourist office.

The holiest *meru* towers have 11 tiers

Because Besakih is one of the island's major attractions, it has become prone to numerous hassles from unofficial 'guides' and other tourist-tracking touts. Local authorities had to step in, and official guides now wear badges and a traditional *endek*-cloth shirt as a uniform. Although theoretically you shouldn't need a guide to simply pay the admission price and walk around the complex with a sarong and sash (stick to the paths, as tourists are not allowed inside any of the temples), you'll be pressured so strongly into taking one that it may be easier to just relent and negotiate the lowest fee you can. Unfortunately, because of all the nuisances, many visitors have

Gunung Agung, Bali's largest and holiest mountain, is often wreathed with clouds

found a trip to Besakih underwhelming – caveat emptor.

Open: daylight hours. Admission charge; guide, camera and parking fees; sarong and sash hire.

Gunung Agung

Legend holds that Gunung Agung was created when the gods split the holy Hindu mountain Meru in two to form it and Batur. Its cloud-crowned peak stands 3,142m (10,308ft) high, and it's the largest mountain on the island, as well as the holiest. All villages and temples are oriented towards it (*see pp84–5*), and many Balinese sleep with their heads towards it as well. It's believed to be the abode of both the gods and the deified souls of Balinese ancestors.

The gods sometimes get angry, though; a massive eruption in 1963 spread mud and molten lava through much of eastern Bali, even down to the sea, killing up to 2,000 people, destroying villages and roads and making 100,000

homeless, many of whom were forced to relocate to other islands. Ash covered all of Bali, wiping out crops and causing widespread famine. It took the island years to recover.

Agung has two main climbing paths: from Selat, on its southwestern slope (at least 3 hours), and from Besakih, which takes 5–7 hours and is much more strenuous. A guide is essential and can be arranged from either point, although in March and April the Besakih route is often unavailable due to religious ceremonies being held there.

Gunung Batur and Gunung Abang

Gunung Batur is one of Bali's most active volcanoes, with more than 20 eruptions in the past 200 years, the last one as recently as 1994. It stands 1,717m (5,633ft) high above an expansive caldera covered with the remains of old lava flows, and is popular for guided sunrise treks (about 2 hours) that leave in pre-dawn darkness. Volcanic activity can sometimes lead to cancellations – even when it's safe, don't be surprised to see smoke coming out of the mountain top – so check with trekking agencies in advance for its current status.

Gunung Abang, just across Danau Batur lake, is a forested mountain 2,152m (7,060ft) high. It's a less popular climb than Batur but its tree cover provides shade and it still affords excellent views. The trek is about 5 hours return, and doesn't need a guide, but it is strenuous. As always, be sure to let someone know your whereabouts, and avoid climbs during rainy season.

Iseh and Sidemen

The winding road south of Selat and Duda on Agung's southwest slope takes you through these two villages and past the loveliest rice-paddy views in the east. Iseh was the home of Walter Spies and Theo Meier, two of the many expatriate artists in pre-war Bali, and in Sidemen you can see *songket* (gold brocade) or *endek* (ikat cloth) being woven on foot looms at its textile workshop.

Penelokan

Penelokan means 'Looking Place', and indeed it's known for its majestic views of Gunung Batur and surrounds. The hawkers run thick here, though, and the lunch-buffet restaurants along the main road are rather soulless. It's also the gateway to the crater towns, with an entrance fee that's collected inconsistently.

Pura Kehen

This state temple of Bangli (Bali's only land-locked district) is one of the largest and most striking of the eastern temples. The hillside setting features a *kulkul* tower in the branches of a massive banyan tree, Chinese porcelain set into the stone walls and an 11-tiered *meru* dedicated to Siwa.
Bangli, 18km (11 miles) directly south of Penelokan. Open: daylight hours. Donation for sarong and sash hire.

Danau Batur lake sits at the base of Gunung Batur

Bali's temples

Bali has at least 20,000 temples – not counting the private temples for worshipping ancestors that are built into every family's compound – and all are significant and sacred to the devout Balinese.

The word for temple, *pura*, comes from the Sanskrit for 'fortress'. Villages and temples are laid out not by the cardinal directions, but by the spatial orientation of Balinese cosmology: 'holy' *kaja*, or upstream, points towards the holy mountain Agung, where the gods live; 'unclean' *kelod*, or downstream, towards the sea, home of evil demons; and *kangin-kauh*, east-west, based on the rising and setting of the sun, symbolises birth and death. The holiest direction is *kaja-kangin*, but since *kaja* always points towards Gunung Agung, in southern Kuta it would point to the northeast corner, in northern Lovina, to the southeast.

Every village, even the smallest, has to build at least three temples: the *pura puseh*, 'temple of origin', which is dedicated to the community founders and to Brahma, the god of creation, and built at the *kaja* end of the village; the *pura desa*, the 'village temple', located in the centre and dedicated to Wisnu, god of life; and the *pura dalem*, the 'temple of the dead', which is set at the *kelod* end of the village, often next to the cemetery, and

Family temples have shrines to the souls of ancestors

dedicated to Siwa, god of death and destruction. In addition to these, larger villages will often have other temples worshipping different gods, such as *pura melanting* for the gods of money and business, often found at markets; or *pura subak*, dedicated to Dewi Sri, the goddess of rice, where farmers can give offerings for a good harvest. *Pura danu*, or lake temples, are dedicated to Dewi Danu, the goddess of the lake, who provides water for irrigating the rice fields.

Besides all of these, there are also nine *kayangan jagat*, or directional temples, usually built in places of great natural beauty, such as a coastline, a mountain or lakeshore. These are the most sacred temples on the island and belong to all Balinese, not just those who live in the area. The *kayangan jagat* protect the island from the evil forces coming from different directions:

- Besakih (*see pp81–2*), on Gunung Agung (central)
- Pura Goa Lawah (*see p77*), near Padang Bai (southeast)
- Pura Lempuyang Luhur, on Gunung Lempuyang (east)
- Pura Luhur Batukaru (*see p68*), on Gunung Batukaru (west)
- Pura Luhur Uluwatu (*see pp45–6*), on Bukit Badung (southwest)
- Pura Masceti, near Gianyar (south)
- Pura Pasar Agung, on Gunung Agung (northeast)

Balinese temples are ornately carved and elaborately decorated

- Pura Ulun Danu Batur (*see p86*), at Danau Batur (north)
- Pura Ulun Danu Bratan (*see p98*), at Danau Bratan (northwest).

Besakih, known as the 'mother temple', is actually a complex of almost 30 separate temples and is the holiest religious site on Bali, drawing hundreds of thousands of visitors every year for the constant ceremonies, which can make for fascinating viewing. But ceremonies are held regularly on Bali at nearly all temples, so enquire at a hotel or tourist office if you'd like to attend one. As it's a formal occasion, you'll need to wear modest clothing and a sarong and sash.

Pura Ulun Danu Batur

The second-most important temple on Bali after Besakih, and one of its nine directional temples (*see pp84–5*), Ulun Danu Batur is dedicated to Dewi Danu, goddess of the lake that provides water for much of the island. Originally built on the lakeshore, the entire temple was moved to the crater rim near Kintamani after Batur's 1926 eruption nearly buried it in lava. There are over 100 shrines to deities great and small, including a large, 11-tiered *meru* for the lake goddess and the god of Gunung Agung.

4km (2¹/₂ miles) north of Penelokan. Open: daylight hours. Admission charge; sarong and sash hire.

A local woman gathering seaweed on Lembongan island

Toya Bungkah

Located 8km (5 miles) down a winding road from Penelokan, this lakeside town at the base of Gunung Batur is the starting point for most treks. There are a number of trekking agencies and modest *losmen* with restaurants serving fresh-caught lake fish.

NUSA LEMBONGAN

Some 20km (12 miles) east of Sanur, Nusa Lembongan island is a popular destination that can be visited on a day trip, but merits a longer stay. More easily accessible and more developed than its larger neighbour Nusa Penida (*see 'Getting away from it all', p122*), it boasts some of the best diving in Indonesia, good waves for surfers and some lovely beaches, albeit with colder water than around Bali.

Plenty of day-trip packages from Bali, focusing on water sports that hardly let you set foot on the island, are on offer, but you can also travel independently with the private transport company Perama or much quicker with the Scoot speedboat that makes the crossing from Sanur to Jungutbatu twice daily in 40 minutes.

Jungutbatu is the settlement on the northern coast, and it's immediately obvious that seaweed production is the main activity; the green and red plants can be seen harvested and drying in the sun everywhere. Several accommodation options can be found along the messy beach,

A secluded white-sand cove near Mushroom Bay, Lembongan island

with more luxurious hotels along the cliffs to the south. For the best beaches, walk 30 minutes along the cliff path via the small Coconut and Chelegimbai beaches to beautiful Mushroom Bay, which can also be reached by motorbike taxi or charter boat. On the southern side of the island, Dream Beach is a quieter option.

Divers flock to Nusa Lembongan for the exceptionally clean water, undisturbed corals and the chance of seeing sharks, mantas and the largest fish on earth, the ocean sunfish, or *mola mola*. Several local and many mainland dive centres organise trips around the island. Snorkelling is best done in Mushroom Bay.

Perama. Tel: (081) 2464 2890.
www.peramatour.com
Scoot Cruise. Tel: (0361) 285 522.
www.scootcruise.com. Open: 8am–8pm.

SEAWEED FARMING

Seaweed aquaculture is big business on Nusa Lembongan and Nusa Penida islands; it overshadows tourism as the main source of income for the islanders. Some 70,000 tons (154 million pounds) of the stuff is produced here each year. Grown on nets suspended in shallow water with bamboo sticks, the green and red seaweed is harvested and laid out in the sun on the beach to dry before it is exported. The seaweed is valuable for its carrageenan, highly flexible gel-like molecules that are used in products as diverse as shampoo, toothpaste, ice cream, beer, fire-fighting foam and sexual lubricants.

North and west Bali

For a change from the touristy feel of southern Bali, a refreshing contrast can be found in Bali's far west and north coast. The confluence of geographical remoteness, differing geology and outside cultural influences has created regions quite distinct from their southern and eastern neighbours, offering travellers the chance to explore some of Bali's least-visited areas and its best coral-reef diving and snorkelling sites.

History

Bali's earliest inhabitants lived in its remote western regions, and proximity to Java made it the entry point for the Hindu priests and aristocracy who would later claim the island for their own. The northern kingdom of Buleleng had a long history of foreign trade through its busy port of Singaraja and fought fiercely against Dutch invasions in the mid-19th century, but became one of the first to fall to colonial occupation. Singaraja spent a century as Bali's capital for both

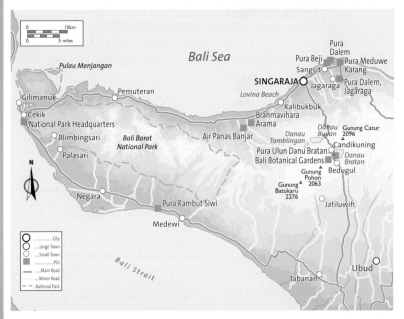

A nudibranch (sea slug) feeding on a reef off Pemuteran

the Dutch and the Republic of Indonesia, until the government was moved to Denpasar in 1953. Recent years have seen an increase in Muslim populations.

Orientation

Bali's west points towards Java, less than 3km (2 miles) across the Bali Strait from Gilimanuk, where a 24-hour ferry runs between the two islands. Bali's only national park comprises most of the mountainous central areas, with towns and villages distributed along its rugged, arid coasts. In the north, Singaraja is the island's second-largest city, but the best base for visitors is nearby Lovina. To the south of Singaraja, the higher inland region around Bedugul has some notable mountains and lakes. Driving from Kuta to Lovina takes around 3 hours.

THE FAR WEST

The remote, mountainous regions of the far west areas of the Buleleng and Jembrana districts are the least populated in Bali, not least because 70 per cent of the land belongs to the island's only national park. With the exception of the beautiful and justifiably popular dive sites at Pulau Menjangan, most of this region is infrequently visited by foreigners and so tourist facilities are limited. Intrepid travellers looking for the unbeaten track can still find a few gems here, though.

Bali Barat National Park

This beautiful national park is discussed in 'Getting away from it all' (*see pp123–4*).

Palasari and Blimbingsari

These villages in the inland jungles of Bali's far west are home to the two main Christian communities on Bali, their adherents relocated in 1939 by the

An open-air bedroom in a Balinese-style bungalow, Pemuteran

Dutch to relieve the antagonism between Christian converts and the majority Hindu population. Blimbingsari is home to the mother church for Bali's roughly 10,000 Protestants, while nearby Palasari, with a population of about 1,500, has the island's only Catholic cathedral and monastery. As both missions purposefully combine Christianity and Balinese culture, the churches display an interesting blend of Balinese-Hindu and Western architecture. Services are held early on most Sunday mornings; call ahead to confirm if you'd like to attend. *Protestant church. Tel: (0365) 421 92. Catholic church. Tel: (0365) 422 01.*

Pemuteran

This small village has great snorkelling and diving in the coral reefs just offshore, where you can see the results of the 'Biorock' artificial reef project (*www.globalcoral.org*) that has been successfully regrowing the coral previously lost due to human negligence and environmental factors. Other activities include swimming in the calm waters off the black-sand beach, horse riding, and hiking in Bali Barat National Park (*see pp123–4*). There are a few rather smart hotels here with plush traditional bungalows, so you can enjoy Pemuteran's quiet atmosphere in style.

Pulau Menjangan

A tiny, uninhabited island 8km (5 miles) off the coast and officially part of the national park, Pulau Menjangan (Deer Island) is surrounded by pristine coral reefs that offer some of the best snorkelling and diving sites to be found on Bali. Seven different locations offer steep wall dives, clear visibility and masses of marine life such as sea urchins, surgeonfish, trumpet fish, parrot fish, barracuda, manta rays, sea turtles and dolphins. Day trips are offered from resort areas all over the island, but the most convenient and cheapest ones can be arranged in nearby Pemuteran or in Lovina, only an hour's ride away.

Pura Rambut Siwi

Niratha, the 16th-century Hindu priest who built the sea temples at Uluwatu and Tanah Lot, stopped at this spot on the rugged southwest coast of Bali and preached his doctrine to the local

THE GREAT HINDU EPICS

Many Balinese narratives come from two ancient epics regarding Hindu morality. The *Ramayana* tells the story of virtuous Prince Rama, sent into exile by his scheming stepmother. His loving wife Sita is later abducted by the demon king Rawana, whom Rama finally defeats with his loyal brother Laksmana and the monkey king Hanuman. The *Mahabharata* concerns a battle for the throne between the good Pandawa brothers (led by Arjuna) and their evil cousins, the Korawas. Ambivalent about fighting, Arjuna turns to his friend Krishna (actually an avatar of Vishnu) who declaims at length on the importance of caste, duty, *karma* and destiny. His faith restored, Arjuna leads his brothers to victory.

villagers, presenting them with a lock of his hair when he left. They soon erected this 'temple for worshipping the hair' (*rambut* means 'hair', as in *rambutan*, 'hairy fruit') on the rocky coast,

North and west Bali

The clear waters off Pulau Menjangan, with western Bali in the distance

enshrining the eponymous tress in the central *meru* tower. It's the most important temple in the entire western district.

Open: daylight hours. Donation for sarong and sash hire.

THE NORTH COAST

The dividing line of volcanoes and lower rainfall means the northern coast sees more dry-land crops, like grapes and coffee, and fewer rice paddies than the south. It also felt the yoke of colonial conquest earliest when the local Buleleng kingdom fell to the Dutch almost 60 years before the rest of the island. Most visitors go north for the appealingly low-key resort area of Lovina, an ideal base for diving trips.

Lovina

Lovina, on the northern coast of Bali, comprises 8km (5 miles) of black-sand beach stretching through six quiet fishing villages and is the largest resort after the Kuta area – yet it couldn't be more different in atmosphere or style. There's less shopping, the beach isn't exciting, the water is too calm for surfing and the nightlife is limited, but visitors looking for a quiet, uncrowded, inexpensive place to relax will find the charm of Lovina hard to resist, even during its busier seasons.

Beyond lazing by the pool or getting a massage at a local spa, there are cookery classes at local restaurants, nearby sites for day trips, safe

THE STORY OF MEN AND PAN BRAYUT

An old Balinese folktale tells the story of Men (Mother) and Pan (Father) Brayut, a poor couple saddled with 18 unmanageable children. Various versions assign the blame differently: in one, Men Brayut picks fights with her husband when she's hungry (which is always), and afterwards they make up the old-fashioned way; in another, Pan Brayut has an insatiable appetite for his wife, which he regularly acts upon. Both work strenuously to support the family and do the household chores, and finally, after all the children are grown, they leave their home and all earthly possessions behind and retire to a spiritual retreat to live out their lives in peace.

swimming on the beach (although no lifeguards) and water sports, fishing and sailing available. The offshore diving and snorkelling areas pale in comparison to those at Pulau Menjangan and Tulamben, but Lovina is a good base for arranging day trips to these from the local dive centres.

The other local tourist activity – heavily advertised and touted – is called 'dolphin watching', but in reality consists of heading out at dawn in one of a dozen noisy motorboats, and chasing after any sighting of the poor, distressed creatures as soon as they surface for air.

History

The last king of the Buleleng regency recognised the area's potential for tourism and built the first tourist hotel here at Kaliasem in the 1960s. Realising the power of name-branding, he called the area 'Lovina' for 'LOVely INdonesiA'.

Orientation

The six villages of the Lovina resort line up along the main road, Jalan Raya Singaraja, from east to west as follows: Pemaron, Tukad Mungga, Anturan, Kalibukbuk, Kaliasem and Temukus. Kalibukbuk is the largest village and the centre of Lovina, with the greatest number of accommodation choices and restaurants available, generally on the main road and around the village centre streets of Jalan Bina Ria and Jalan Mawar, as well as on the side road called Banyualit, just 1.5km (1 mile) to the east. *Bemos* run east-west along the main road during the day; by night you'll need to use your own transport or, if you've been drinking, one of the many touts. Motorbikes and bicycles are easily hired around Lovina, but be careful on the busy main road.

Kaliasem

Just east of Kalibukbuk, Kaliasem is home to the area's only 5-star PADI dive centre (which also offers water sports), as well as *sapi gerumbungan*, or traditional buffalo races (*see p147*), in high season, advertised on local flyers.

Kalibukbuk

As the centre of Lovina, Kalibukbuk has a number of quite good restaurants, including Thai and Italian among the usual Indonesian fare, as well as some specialising in seafood (locally caught and always fresh). It's also home to most of the area's best bars (the majority of which offer regular live music), the only nightclub in the area, near Banyualit, and a surprisingly fast internet café. A monument to the area's dolphins stands on the beach at the end of Jalan Bina Ria, near a small art market and several beachside cafés.

Fishing boats, Lovina beach

The Air Panas hot springs is a popular bathing spot

Around Lovina
Air Panas Banjar

Take the waters with the locals at this popular bathing site, comprising three pools filled with warm, silky-soft water by a naturally sulphuric hot spring. Also on site are changing rooms and lockers, a restaurant and a spa with an outdoor Jacuzzi® and massages available.
10km (6 miles) southwest of Lovina. Admission charge.

Brahmavihara Arama

Bali's only Buddhist monastery is located just down the road from the hot springs. The beautiful hillside temples offer ocean views and feature classic Thai-style elements such as golden statues and a *stupa* ('monument'). Ten-day meditation

retreats are offered here in April and September, and the site is closed to visitors during those times. If you visit, please dress modestly, use low voices and take your shoes off as directed.
3km (2 miles) from Air Panas. Tel: (0362) 929 54. www.brahmaviharaarama.com. Open: daylight hours. Admission by donation.

Singaraja and around

Singaraja, the second-largest city on Bali, was formerly the Dutch colonial capital and the main gateway for tourists until the ascendance of Kuta as a tourist base, the administrative move to Denpasar and the opening of Ngurah Rai Airport permanently shifted its significance to the south. Its centuries-long history as a bustling trading port for Muslim, Chinese and other Asian merchants is still reflected in the culturally diverse population of approximately 100,000, and its two major universities, a legacy from Dutch reforms, make it the cosmopolitan and intellectual centre of Bali. Singaraja has little to offer tourists besides the famous *lontar* manuscript library and a walk down by the old harbourside, but a number of notable temples can be found in the vicinity.

Gedong Kirtya Library

This library is the only repository of *lontar* palm manuscripts in the world, founded by the Dutch in 1928 to help preserve traditional Balinese culture and atone for their brutal conquests of the previous decades. These 3,000 sacred texts, some with marvellously intricate illustrations, are inscribed on the dried and bound leaves of the *lontar* palm, thus preserving centuries of Balinese customs, medicine, astrology and philosophy. The library also has 10th-century inscribed bronze plates, some of the oldest Balinese writings known to exist.

Jl Veteran 20. Tel: (0362) 226 45. Open: Mon–Thur 9am–4pm, Fri 9am–1pm. Admission charge.

Pura Beji and Pura Dalem, Sangsit

A *subak* (irrigation association) temple dedicated to Dewi Sri, goddess of rice growing, Pura Beji was built in the 15th century in pink sandstone, and is filled with exuberant carvings of animals, demons and symbols of water and fertility. About 400m (¹/₄ mile) across the rice fields is Sangsit's Pura Dalem, or 'Temple of the Dead', which features a front wall depicting heavenly rewards for the virtuous and, more intriguingly, vicious (and rather graphic) punishments being meted out to sinners in hell.

At Sangsit, 9km (6 miles) east of Singaraja. Open: daylight hours. Donation for sarong and sash hire.

Pura Dalem, Jagaraga

Jagaraga was the site of two bloody battles in the Dutch invasions of 1848–9. Although the first battle was

A gilded Buddha at Bali's only Buddhist monastery

won (with heavy losses) by 16,000 Balinese warriors against 3,000 Dutch soldiers, when the Dutch returned ten months later, the Balinese were thoroughly routed and the northern regency of Buleleng finally fell under complete Dutch control. The town's temple of the dead is, perhaps fittingly, dedicated to Siwa (Shiva) the Destroyer, and its front wall features carvings showing Balinese life before and after Dutch colonisation (*see pp100–101*) – peaceful Balinese fishing and flying kites, followed by the Dutch arriving in biplanes, automobiles and steamships – as well as the harried mother of Balinese legend, Men Brayut, being overwhelmed by her numerous children (*see box, p92*).

At Jagaraga, 5km (3 miles) south of Sangsit. Open: daylight hours. Admission by donation.

The famous 'bicycle man' carving, Pura Meduwe Karang

Pura Meduwe Karang

This large, ornately carved temple, dedicated to the god who oversees crops grown on non-irrigated land (such as fruit or coffee), is widely considered to be the finest in the area. The wall carvings include characters from the Hindu epic *Ramayana* and various Balinese people such as *legong* dancers, but it's most famous for the whimsical depiction of a man on a bicycle, meant to be the Dutch artist W O J Nieuwenkamp, who explored Bali on two wheels in 1904.

At Kubutambahan, 11km (7 miles) east of Singaraja. Open: daylight hours. Donation for sarong and sash hire.

AROUND BEDUGUL

The mountainous area around Bedugul is generally more of a draw for domestic tourists than foreign ones, but does have a number of pleasant attractions off the beaten path, including some small towns, picturesque lakes, one of Bali's holiest temples, a large botanical garden and a golf course located inside a volcanic crater. Temperatures here are quite a bit cooler than in the coastal areas, especially at night, and conditions can be rainier and more overcast, so have warmer clothing handy if touring the area.

Bali Botanical Gardens

Opened in 1959, these 150-hectare (370-acre) Botanical Gardens on the slopes of Gunung Pohon (Tree

Mountain) were Indonesia's first, and are home to over 1,700 plant species, including more than 650 different trees and almost 500 kinds of orchids. Bird-watching enthusiasts will want to keep their eyes open for some of the 100 different bird species here, including barbets, parrots, starlings and kingfishers. It's a popular picnic spot, with busier crowds on weekends, especially when the weather's fine. A booklet of six self-guided walks can be purchased at the ticket office, or you can drive your vehicle around the grounds. There's also a herbarium, collections of roses, cacti and bamboo, views of Danau Bratan and three temples.
At Candikuning. Tel: (0368) 212 73. Open: 8am–5pm. Admission and vehicle charge.

Candikuning

Nestled against the northwestern shore of Lake Bratan, this small market town is a fine place to stop for lunch. The daily market at Bukit Mungsu offers spices, plants and some of the tropical flowers and fruit that are grown in the cool temperatures and volcanic soil around here. The area is known for its local strawberries, which are used to make fresh milkshakes, ice cream and pancakes at local cafés. There's a large Muslim population here, so you may see differences in local dress and food options. Several kilometres up the road is the Bali Handara Kosaido Country Club (*see p169*), one of Bali's most beautiful golf courses and the only one in the world located inside the caldera of a volcano.

North and west Bali

With views of Danau Bratan, the Botanical Gardens are popular with picnickers

Bali has the only golf course in the world located in a volcano's crater

Danau Bratan and Pura Ulun Danu Bratan

This large, deep lake sits serenely at the base of Gunung Catur, 1,200m (4,000ft) above sea level. It's a popular site with domestic visitors, especially with the water sports and boat rentals available from the recreational park on the southern shore (*see p169*).

Because the lake is the main water source for many of Bali's rice paddies, the goddess of the lake, Dewi Danu, is worshipped here at the temple complex on the western shore, built in 1633 by the king of Mengwi. It's also one of the nine sacred directional temples of Bali (*see pp84–5*), protecting the northwest part of Bali, and one of the most visited and photographed temples on the island.

It's easy to see why: the *meru* towers are located on small islets near the shore and seem to be almost suspended above the placid waters. Originally they were indeed surrounded by water and reachable only by boat, but water levels have dropped due to environmental mismanagement in the area and the temples are now on dry land. Still, when the clouds drop low between the temple and Gunung Catur, it's a quietly stunning sight. There's also a restaurant and small market off the car park.
Open: daylight hours. Admission charge.

Danau Buyan and Danau Tamblingan

Approximately 6km (3³/₄ miles) north of Danau Bratan is Danau Buyan, separated from the smaller Danau Tamblingan to its west by a narrow strip of land, created by a landslide in the 19th century that divided the once-larger lake in two. A road through the coastal villages winds around to the southern end of Danau Tamblingan, offering beautiful views from various vantage points, and there are also some good trekking trails around the lakes leading to the various temples on their shores. Don't stray from them as it's easy to get lost in the dense woods.

Gunung Catur

At 2,096m (6,877ft), Gunung Catur (also called Gunung Mangu) is one of the easier mountains on Bali to climb without a guide, with a path that starts close to the shore of Danau Bratan near the Taman Rekreasi Bedugul. The trail runs through shaded forest areas and should take about 2–3 hours of steady hiking to reach the top, with a small temple and fantastic lake views at the summit. It does get fairly steep as you reach the top, however, so should only be attempted by the very fit. Be sure to bring plenty of water and snacks and let someone know where you're going beforehand, and be sure to take the same trail back. Visitors are strongly advised not to attempt a climb in the rainy season.

Pura Ulun Danu Bratan sits serenely among the clouds

The colonial past

The colonial past of Bali and Lombok starts with spices. Until the 16th century, Arab and Indian traders had dominated the trade routes between Southeast Asia and Europe, shipping large and extremely valuable quantities of pepper, nutmeg and clove west and bringing Islam to Indonesia.

First contact

The Portuguese were the first to venture out to India and Indonesia in the 16th century to take over some of the trade, but they later concentrated on other areas, leaving Indonesia to the Dutch. Over a period of three centuries, the Dutch East India Company (a commercial company with shareholders – arguably the first ever multinational enterprise) gradually took control of Indonesia, using local trade alliances rather than military force to gain access. In 1816, the Dutch government took over the colony, now named the Dutch East Indies, focusing on plantations, mining and oil.

Bali

The Dutch first came to Bali in the 1830s, but after negotiations to take over the island failed, they sent in the military three times between 1846 and 1849, causing heavy casualties among the troops of the Balinese *rajas* ('kings'). It was during these skirmishes that the *raja* of Karangasem commited *puputan*, a suicidal fight to the death, together

The statue at Puputan Square commemorates the ritual suicide of the last king of Badung and his court

with his family. The whole entourage dressed up in their finest clothes and walked straight into the line of fire, with their own people finishing off the wounded with their sharp *keris* (daggers). In July 1849 most local *rajas* agreed to Dutch rule in exchange for remaining in charge of their own territories. Dutch control over South Bali was completed in 1909, but not until after more horrific *puputan* in 1906 and 1908. The subsequent colonial period saw the beginnings of tourism on Bali and the settlement of many foreign artists.

Lombok

Eastern Lombok was settled by the Dutch in 1674 with Selong as the administrative capital, though there was little development until the 1891 Sasak revolt against the Balinese who controlled the island. The Dutch used the event to try to take control of Lombok. During this military operation the Balinese struck out by successfully driving back the Dutch army from Cekranegara's Mayura Water Palace to Ampenang, but the Dutch reinforced their troops and came back a few months later, forcing the Balinese to surrender in 1894. Some members of the Balinese royal family, as well as some locals, chose to commit *puputan*, a scene repeated later that year near Lingsar as the last

pocket of resistance was neutralised. After the Dutch takeover, the island was neglected and people on Lombok faced incredible difficulties paying the taxes imposed on them.

Independence

The popular backlash from the *puputan* stories that reached the European and US press caused the Dutch to take a more careful colonial approach afterwards. A so-called 'Ethical Policy' was implemented, shifting focus from exploiting the colonies to enabling the locals to improve their own situation. The Japanese invasion in World War II showed the local population that their colonisers were more vulnerable than they thought, and the Dutch colonial era eventually came to its end as the Netherlands was forced to accept Indonesia's independence in 1949, after a futile four-year military struggle.

The carvings at Jagaraga's Pura Dalem depict the arrival of the Dutch and modern technology

South and west Lombok

Compared to Bali, Lombok doesn't see many foreign tourists, and of those who do make it across the Lombok Strait, the vast majority limit their stay to the islands, resorts and towns in the south and west of the island. Many visitors will arrive at the airport of Mataram, Lombok's distinguished administrative capital. There are a few worthwhile sights in and around the city, but most visitors decide to visit them on day trips.

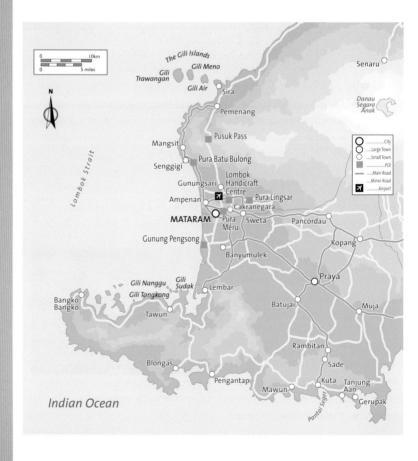

Lombok's only mall, in central Mataram

Senggigi, just a short taxi ride north, is Lombok's busiest beach resort town. Shops, restaurants and travel agencies jostle for space along the coastal road that dips inland here, some excellent resort hotels line the white-sand crescent beaches, and it's the only place on Lombok's mainland with any nightlife to speak of. It's an excellent place to be based for a while and it's possible to make all your Lombok and Bali travel arrangements here.

The three Gili Islands just off Lombok's northwest coast, Gili Air, Gili Meno and Gili Tranwangan, are perfect for lazing on the sand, snorkelling, diving, strolling between the coconut plantations and enjoying sunset dinners on *bale* platforms overlooking the sea.

Kuta, the small fishing village on Lombok's south coast, couldn't be more different from Bali's party town of the same name. Tourists in the know head here for the beautiful, deserted white-sand beaches immediately to the east and west.

MATARAM AND AROUND
Banyumulek
This village specialises in elegant Lombok-style pottery, also often spotted on Bali, which is intricately decorated with woven rattan. The main road in the village is lined with drying clay pots and small craft shops, with the

cottage industry production going on in the back alleys.

9km (5¹/₂ miles) south of Mataram. Shops open: Mon–Sat.

Gunung Pengsong

The temple buildings crowning this hill are nothing special, but the views over the lush plain towards Gunung Rinjani are stunning. Come early or late in the day to avoid cloud cover and the heat – it's a steep climb.

6km (3³/₄ miles) south of Mataram.

Lombok Handicraft Centre

Sayang Sayang crafts village, marked by a large gate, is great for buying crafts, with dozens of shops selling everything from masks to carved decorations and furniture.

2km (1¹/₄ miles) north of Cakranegara. Shops open: Mon–Sat.

Pura Lingsar

Set between lily-filled ponds, this pretty 18th-century temple is famous for being a place of worship for both Hindus and the local Wetu Telu Muslims (who use the lower temple courtyard).

7km (4¹/₃ miles) east of Cakranegara. Donation for sash hire.

Pura Meru and Puri Mayura

Lombok's largest Balinese temple and the main sight in town is the 18th-century Meru temple, with its impressive carved gateway and three consecutive courtyards. Just across the road, the Puri Mayura (Water Palace) has a breezy pavilion in a pretty lake where locals come to picnic, fish and prepare their cockerels for fights.

Jl Selaparang, Cakranegara. Admission charge.

The view from Gunung Pengsong temple

The pagoda of the Pura Meru temple in Cakranegara

SENGGIGI AND MANGSIT

Lombok's main tourist hotspot suffered a lot from the last downturn in tourism, with boarded-up shops, half-empty shopping centres and an abandoned resort. There's no reason to let this spoil the fun, however, as Senggigi is on the rebound, with several new restaurant and bar openings marking the locals' optimistic outlook. The town centre, spread along Jalan Raya Senggigi, is functional rather than attractive, and offers everything you might need, from dining, nightlife and souvenir hunting to travel agent offerings.

Senggigi's two white-sand beaches are separated by a narrow headland with a reef where surfers can often be seen riding the waves. The beach to the north of the headland is partly for sunbathing and partly used by the local fishermen to park and repair their outrigger boats during the day. Come to the beach at sunset to watch them set off to sea for a night of tuna fishing.

LOMBOK'S HAWKERS

Some visitors resent the hawkers, especially in Senggigi and Kuta, who tirelessly work the beaches and streets for potential buyers of their sarongs, massages and bracelets. Keep in mind, however, that Lombok is markedly poorer than Bali, its tourism income was hit as badly as Bali's in recent years, and it's been slower to recover. If you don't want to buy something, just say 'no' politely once or twice. Some hotels, like the Sheraton in Senggigi, have agreed rules of conduct with the hawkers, and they'll be less persistent there.

South of the headland, the beach is long and empty, backed by a few hotels and restaurants, and diligently patrolled by hawkers. For quieter beaches, take a taxi or *bemo* north to Mangsit or beyond, but remember to take food and drinks.

The coastal road

North of Senggigi, the coastal road towards Pemenang is practically void of traffic, and the roller-coaster ride, involving climbing several headlands before descending to the next bay, is rewarded with marvellous views. Most of the bays have pretty coconut-fringed beaches with small fishing communities living nearby, and you can practically claim any beach as your own for the day. Combined with the Pusuk Pass (*see opposite*), this makes an excellent bike or car trip, which can also be combined with a visit to Sira beach (*see p125*).

Mangsit beach

The first of many bays stretching between Senggigi and Pemenang, Mangsit is the most developed yet still serene, with just a few resorts lining the beach. The sand isn't as white as on the Gilis, and the surf can be rather violent, but the snorkelling at the northern part of the beach is quite good. Hire snorkelling gear at the adjacent Windy Beach resort.

Pura Batu Bulong

Senggigi's only real sight is a Hindu temple complex on a headland, named after the large hole in the volcanic rock. Though the temple and shrines are modest, you can stand on the lava flows

A new shopping plaza in central Senggigi

People hopping off the public boat to Gili Trawangan

and take in the beautiful views of two bays with jungle beyond.

1km (²/₃ mile) south of Senggigi. Donation for sash hire.

Pusuk Pass

An easy excursion by car or taxi, the 800m (2,625ft) high pass on the direct route from Mataram to Pemenang is reached via the hectic market town of Gunungsari. As the road climbs, villages are left behind and dense jungle takes over the views. A set of hairpin bends fringed by restaurants offering great views announces the final climb to the pass. At the top you can enjoy views of the lowlands and the Gili Islands through the trees. Monkeys hang around the parking places, expecting handouts from passing drivers.

THE GILI ISLANDS

The three picture-perfect paradise Gili Islands ('Gili' actually meaning island) can be reached by public or chartered

boats from Bangsal, or with Perama's boats from Senggigi or Padang Bai on Bali. Each of the small islands has a slightly different character, with Gili Trawangan best geared for fun and activities, Gili Meno offering peace and quiet, and Gili Air somewhere in between.

You'll soon notice the relaxed atmosphere that makes the islands so popular. There is no motorised traffic at

DIVING AND SNORKELLING AROUND THE GILI ISLANDS

The Gili Islands are famed for their diving and snorkelling opportunities. Even with no experience, it's easy to hire a snorkel and splash around the shallows to spot dozens of species of colourful tropical fish and turtles if you're lucky. Sea warming and strong currents mean that the coral is poor, but the variety of fish life makes up for that. Ask about the prevailing currents first if you plan to set off alone. It's also possible to hop on a glass-bottomed boat tour, which passes over all the main underwater sights around all three islands in half a day.

A horse-cart taxi waits for passengers on Gili Trawangan's main road

all. To get around, you can go on foot, hire a bicycle or hop onto a *cidomo* ('horse-cart'). Going between the islands is easy, either on the twice-daily shuttle ferries, or by inexpensive chartered boats. All three islands have restaurants with beachfront *bale* platforms where you can enjoy the view. The sun rises spectacularly over Lombok's Gunung Rinjani and sets in similar fashion behind Bali's Gunung Agung.

Gili Air

Closest to the mainland, Gili Air is the most populated of the three Gilis. The village centre is near the ferry landing point and stilt-house coconut farms are dispersed across the island and connected by a maze of paths. Gili Air offers better chances than the other islands for chatting with the locals while you wander around the coconut plantations. Its east coast is the most developed, with a smattering of budget guesthouses, restaurants and dive shops scattered along the coral-strewn beach. The northeast tip of the island, 15 minutes' walk from the ferry landing, has some bars and restaurants that serve fresh grilled fish and occasionally throw parties. Wander around to the west coast, however, and you'll probably find yourself alone on the beach. The best beach for sunbathing and snorkelling is on the east coast, where the water is warm and shallow until the drop-off some 30m (98ft) from the beach.

Gili Meno

The middle and smallest of the Gili Islands is also the quietest of all three. It only has a handful of budget guesthouses, food options and diving centres. Inland, there's a small saltwater lake and a bird park. The diving and snorkelling are arguably best around Gili Meno. Just west of the island, the Meno Wall is a diver's paradise, and turtle sightings are almost guaranteed here.

Gili Trawangan

'Gili T', as Trawangan island is nicknamed by party-goers, is the furthest from the mainland and has the most facilities. The road along its east coast is lined with dozens of guesthouses, bars, restaurants and diving centres, and though it's not as quiet as the other two islands, it's relaxed nevertheless. The pleasant beach is shaded with casuarina trees and offers good snorkelling off the east coast, with another good diving spot to the northwest of the island. All divers contribute a small amount to the island's eco-trust, which pays for security guards and the coral regeneration project.

As on Gili Meno and Gili Air, the west coast of Gili T is practically deserted and you're advised to take sufficient water if you plan to walk around the island. The island's central village with its school and mosque makes for a leisurely walk or horse ride, while the hill in the middle of Gili Trawangan is a popular place to see the sun set over Bali's Gunung Agung.

As well as a good range of *warung* and restaurants, Gili Trawangan has some of Lombok's best nightlife options. Especially during high season, backpackers fill the bars which take turns in hosting parties, so there's a different place to go every night. There is even a night-time shuttle boat from Gili Air to bring revellers here.

KUTA

Some 50km (31 miles) south of Mataram along good roads lies the small, ramshackle fishing village of Kuta, quite a different place from Bali's version. Several hotels and guesthouses can be found along the roads immediately to the west and east. It's usually very quiet, and the best time to visit is on Sunday mornings, when *bemos* and motorbikes jostle for space

Gili Air's coral-strewn beach, with views of the sunset behind Mt Agung

Farmers selling tobacco at Kuta's Sunday market

around the lively weekly market, which attracts hundreds of people from surrounding villages. Tropical fruit, vegetables, fish, tofu, clothes, exotic snacks, Lombok peppers and tobacco are all for sale.

Mawun

Driving west from Kuta, the reasonably good coastal road climbs a steep hill to a restaurant from where there are stunning views over Kuta and the beaches and bays beyond. Some 8km (5 miles) further, an asphalt road turning left leads you to glorious Mawun beach, a perfect crescent of white sand and blue water framed by two green hills. Guarded parking is available, though there are no other facilities.

Rambitan and Sade

Two traditional Sasak villages along the main road between Mataram and Kuta can easily be visited. Tiny Rambitan is 7km (4^1/$_3$ miles) north of Kuta and is the more worthwhile one. A tour will take you past family homes, the characteristic *lumbung* rice storage huts and the Masjid Kuno mosque, the oldest on Lombok. Sade village, 2km (1^1/$_4$ miles) closer to Kuta, is larger and more modern, with paved paths and a village square. The locals here are quite used to seeing tourists wander around, and many make some extra money by selling souvenirs from their homes. Walk down back alleys past the thatched mosque to find quieter village scenes. The best time to visit Rambitan and Sade is in the early morning or late afternoon when the villagers are at home.
Admission by donation.

Tanjung Aan and beyond

East of Kuta, the road infrastructure for new resort hotels is already in place, though just one has been built so far. The best place for sunbathing and swimming is 4km (2^1/$_2$ miles) from Kuta at Tanjung Aan bay, where a long crescent of shadeless white sand overlooks the light blue water. There are two spots with guarded parking and refreshments, and some hawkers on the beach, but otherwise the beach is completely devoid of development, so you're best to take your own snacks and drinks.

Tanjung Aan and adjacent Pantai Seger beach are the most important sites for the annual religious *Bau Nyale* festival (every February or March), when millions of Nyale sea worms spawn for just one day after the full moon. The legend goes that Princess Putri Mandalika jumped into the sea to avoid having to choose between several suitors. Locals believe the worms to be a manifestation of the princess, and hope for aphrodisiac effects by eating the worms raw or grilled. Plenty of worms are also seen as a good omen for the rice harvest.

Driving past Tanjung Aan, you'll arrive at the end of the road in dusty Gerupak village, which is popular with surfers for the breaks that are visible in the distance. A small surfer's bar and restaurant overlooks the outrigger boats in the bay.

South and west Lombok

A bird's-eye view of Kuta's bay and beaches

North and east Lombok

Far from the crowds, North Lombok is the driest and least populated part of the island. The area south of massive Gunung Rinjani (Mount Rinjani, Indonesia's second-highest volcano) is lush and green due to the rains which mainly fall on this side of the mountain. From Pemenang, the town closest to the Gili Islands, the coastal road twists and turns its way east through cashew-nut plantations and past volcanic pumice-stone quarries.

See pp118–19 for drive route.

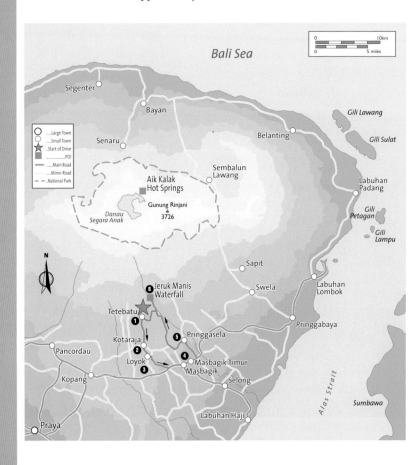

There are several sights here that make a worthy excursion or multi-day trip from Senggigi, including the authentic Sasak village of Segenter and the old mosque at Bayan, but most visitors head straight for the cool air of Senaru village, the starting point for Gunung Rinjani hikes and also less strenuous walks around the paddy fields and waterfalls. The large hanging valley directly east of the mountain is deliciously cool and offers scenic walks around Sembalun Lawang. Further east, the coast is little explored and not well geared towards tourists, but there are some good beaches, snorkelling and diving.

North Lombok is a poor area, and visitors can help by making use of the guided tours through the Sasak villages; your donations benefit the whole community. South of the mountain, Tetebatu sits high amid stunningly green and unspoiled rice-paddy

The Tiu Kelep waterfall near Senaru

terraces, and is a great base for walking around the fields, visiting local markets, exploring the many crafts villages in the immediate surroundings and walking through the rainforest to the impressive Jeruk Manis waterfall.

SASAK FAITH

Some 85 per cent of Lombok's population is Sasak, a culture with its own religion and a language similar to Balinese. Most Sasaks are Muslims, though many follow the Wetu Telu faith, which is different from orthodox Islam in the number of daily prayers (*wetu telu* means 'three times') and in its incorporation of older animist beliefs. Over the past century, many Sasaks have been converted to the more orthodox Wetu Lima ('five times'), but a few thousand remaining Bodha Sasaks in highland villages have resisted all conversion attempts and still practise an ancient religion that is a mix of Hinduism, Buddhism and animism.

THE NORTH AND EAST COAST

Bayan

Reached by turning inland at Anyar along steeply ascending roads, this village sits on the northern extent of the rice fields, fed by runoff from Gunung Rinjani, which towers immediately behind. Bayan is known as the birthplace of the Sasak's Wetu Telu religion, and you can visit the impressive 300-year-old thatched mosque and a small traditional village set amid beautiful paddy fields.

Labuhan Padang and the east-coast islands

Just north of the eastern harbour town of Labuhan Lombok, the village of Labuhan Padang has a pleasant beach and is a port for those who want to venture to the islands of Gili Petagan, Gili Sulat, Gili Lawang and tiny Gili Lampu. There are no facilities on these islands, but you can expect deserted white-sand beaches, dense mangrove forests and some great undisturbed snorkelling and diving spots. Gear and boats can be hired from Labuhan Padang, and some Senggigi dive centres also do trips here.

Segenter

Signposted 3km (2 miles) down a narrow road through parched landscapes some 12km (7¹/₂ miles)

Villagers relaxing in Segenter, a traditional Sasak village

west of Bayan, Segenter is one of Lombok's most authentic Sasak villages and is well worth a visit. A local guide will meet you at the entrance and show you around for a small fee. Some 350 people live here, each family inhabiting a standard-design thatched hut with mud floors. Each hut has separate levels for cooking and sleeping, with a wooden interior room for rice storage which doubles as a honeymoon suite during a couple's first three nights of marriage. Foreign NGOs have done much to improve living standards, constructing water pipes, a school, toilets and washing areas.

Sembalun Lawang

Situated in a beautiful hanging valley between high volcanic peaks, this village is famed for its garlic and other market garden crops which do well in the fertile soil. It is reached by a very steep asphalt road from the north coast, and you can drive south from here across Lombok's highest pass (occasionally closed due to landslides) and down through dense rainforest to Sapit. Hikers planning to scale Gunung Rinjani's summit often start here. Non-climbers can join guided walks by RTC (see p172). Their half-day village walk passes local farms, bamboo gardens and coffee trees, and goes up a hill for views over the mountain and the coast. On their easy two-day 'wildflowers walk', a porter and guide accompany you through tropical forests to grasslands where orchids and other flowers carpet the ground.

Senaru

Senaru, a mountain village set 600m (2,000ft) high up on the flanks of Gunung Rinjani, is noticeably cooler than the coastal area, and makes for a pleasant stay even if you're not planning to climb the volcano. As part of a project aiming to increase employment for the local population, local women can take you on guided walks through the paddy fields and plantations. Walks start from the pretty traditional Sasak settlement at the top of the road and also take in two impressive jungle waterfalls, Sindang Gila and Tiu Kelep.

GUNUNG RINJANI NATIONAL PARK

Founded in 1977 and centred around the 3,726m (12,224ft) high volcano, Gunung Rinjani National Park covers 450sq km (174sq miles), holds 85 per cent of the surviving forests on Lombok and is open from May to October. Local legend tells of Princess Dewa Rinjani, daughter of King Datu Tuan and Queen Dewi Mas, who had been separated for years after a misunderstanding. The princess went up the mountain to meditate and was asked by the mountain spirits to become their leader, and as a result Gunung Rinjani was named after her. Locals of both the Hindu and Wetu Telu religions hold the mountain sacred, and regular pilgrimages to the crater lake take place.

The volcano was formed a million years ago above the spot where two tectonic plates meet. Rinjani was originally much higher, but massive eruptions 14,000 years ago caused the collapse of the mountain and the formation of the current caldera valley and lake. Several small, younger volcanic cones have since formed inside the caldera. The Gunung Baru volcano inside the caldera last erupted in 1994, heating up the lake from 18 to 40°C (64 to 104°F), and causing mud streams that killed 31 people. The volcano is now considered safe to climb.

The various climate levels on the mountain are home to an incredible diversity of plant and animal life. Some 425 species of plants have been counted, several of them endemic to the mountain. Animal species include long-tailed grey macaque and ebony leaf monkeys, wild pigs and barking deer.

The stunning view over Gunung Rinjani's crater lake

Walk: Gunung Rinjani

The route up Indonesia's second-highest volcano is one of Southeast Asia's most beautiful and rewarding treks. The walk to the crater rim and back takes two days, and you'll need four days to go to the summit and back. The hike is long and steep but most fit people can do at least the stretch to the crater rim. Guides and porters can be arranged at fairly short notice, and the price includes food, water, tents, sleeping bags and park admission. Trips booked in Senggigi or Mataram include all additional road transport.

1 Senaru, 600m (1,968ft)

Hikers set off early in the morning from the Rinjani Trek Centre office near the Sasak village at the top of the road (*see also p115*).

2 Rinjani crater rim, 2,650m (8,695ft)

Passing two resting areas and taking time for drinking in the views, slow-paced hikers reach the crater rim after about 7 hours. The track goes through virgin rainforest and the temperature drops as you climb. The night is spent at the camping ground near the crater rim, and in the early morning at sunrise when the skies are always clear you have dazzling views over the massive caldera (the part of the volcano that collapsed to form a high-altitude valley now filled with a lake), Lombok's north coast and Bali. Two-day hikers return to Senaru here, others continue to the lake.

3 Segara Anak lake and hot springs, 2,050m (6,725ft)

It's two hours of steep downhill walking to the crater lake shore. The lake is considered sacred by Lombok's inhabitants, and is a pilgrimage destination. Completely surrounded by the towering volcano rim and forested with alpine-looking pine trees and even edelweiss, it's truly a magical landscape, and some visitors choose to relax here for a day or two. Poking out from the waters is the perfect cone of Gunung Baru (2,363m/7,753ft), which last erupted in 1994. You can make your way up there, or just settle for a swim in the lake, exploring some caves or soaking in the nearby Aik Kalak hot springs.

4 Gunung Rinjani summit, 3,726m (12,224ft)

Hardy types can attempt the hike from the second rim camping site up to the summit, a steep 3-hour climb undertaken at night so you arrive just in time for sunrise. The views from this height are stunning; you can see all of Lombok and the neighbouring islands.

5 Sembalun Lawang, 1,150m (3,773ft)

An alternative starting or finishing point which makes for a shorter hike to the rim is the cool and pleasant highland village of Sembalun Lawang (*see p114*).

6 Aik Buka, 500m (1,640ft)

Nature enthusiasts should not skip the opportunity to hike the recently opened path leading up from the village of Aik Buka on Rinjani's southern flank. The path is difficult but cuts through dense virgin rainforest, and animal sightings are more common here than on other routes. RTC (*see p172*) arranges hikes starting from here, which also include a rafting trip on the lake.

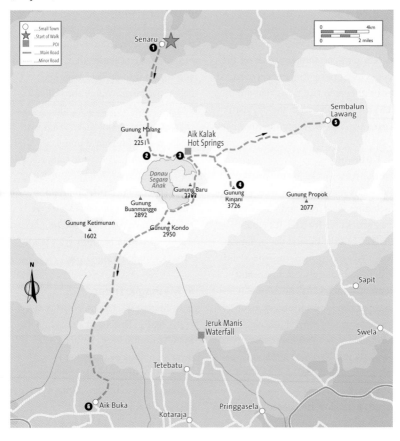

Drive: Tetebatu and the crafts villages

This 40km (25-mile) car or bike trip takes you through unspoiled landscapes with rice paddies and tobacco fields, passing several crafts villages. The drive can be started at any point, though it's recommended to visit the Kotaraja market in the morning.

Allow at least half a day for the drive.

See map p112 for route.

1 Tetebatu

Some 50km (31 miles) northeast of Mataram, Tetebatu village, with its selection of guesthouses, is set on the slopes of Gunung Rinjani, surrounded by bright green rice fields that are used for growing tobacco in the dry season.
Drive 3km (2 miles) south to Kotaraja.

2 Kotaraja

Stock up on snacks for the day at Kotaraja's market, where local produce including *salak* fruit and *plosor* rice cake snacks are for sale. It's a daily market, but the busiest day is Sunday when villagers from across the island visit. Kotaraja is also an important centre for metal, and functional items like gates and farm tools are made at the blacksmiths' workshops near the mosque.
Drive 4km (2¹/₂ miles) south to Loyok.

3 Loyok

Locals here have specialised in bamboo weaving. A few shops selling the full range of woven bamboo articles can be found near the central crossroads. Bamboo is repeatedly split until it is nearly as thin as paper, then it's painted and woven into baskets, bags and decorative boxes. Watch the skilled weavers make *anyaman bambu* (*ngulat tereng* in Sasak), a woven mat customised with your name.
Turn left at the Loyok crossroads, right at the next one, drive through Rungkang, turn left onto the busy main road in Paokmetong, pass through Masbagik town and turn right further east down a signposted road to Masbagik Timur, 9km (5¹/₂ miles) from Loyok.

4 Masbagik Timur

'East Masbagik' is a renowned pottery crafts centre. Dozens of shops line the road here, all selling characteristic brown Lombok pottery that is decorated with eggshells and woven bamboo. Ask to be shown the backstreet pottery workshops where the pots are made and baked.

Continue east on the main road, turning left and reaching Pringgasela after 5km (3 miles).

5 Pringgasela

Near the main crossroads in the centre of the village you'll see a few shops selling traditionally woven products. The wide, patterned ikat cloths are made on large standing looms, while *songkets* are narrower, have linear patterns and are woven on small hand looms. Ask around to be shown how the women weave *songkets*.

Follow signs west to Jurit, turn right after 2km (1¹/₄ miles), and right again towards Kembang Kuning after another

2km (1¹/₄ miles), at the mosque in Lendang Nangka. Turn right after another 6km (3³/₄ miles) and left after another 2km (1¹/₄ miles).

6 Jeruk Manis waterfall

Just inside the boundaries of the Gunung Rinjani National Park, this impressive 20m (66ft) high waterfall plunges from a cliff into a shaded pool surrounded by lush green foliage. It is reached via an easy 1.5km (1-mile) path heading up through forest and past a few picnic spots.

Parking and admission charge. Return to Kembang Kuning and turn right to reach Tetebatu after 1km (²/₃ mile).

Drive: Tetebatu and the crafts villages

A weaver making a traditional *songket* in Pringgasela

Getting away from it all

Bali's cities, Denpasar and Singaraja, are not really tourist destinations, and most of its resorts are quite close to rural areas – getting away from it all here isn't about leaving the urban behind, but simply getting further from the madding crowd of tourist-heavy regions. There are a number of quieter areas of Bali and Lombok where you can feel less like a walking wallet and more like a welcomed guest or an intrepid explorer.

BALI

Amed

Amed, a string of sleepy little fishing villages on Bali's unspoiled eastern coast, used to be one of Bali's best-kept secrets. But even though word has started to get out about the relaxed pace, beautiful coral-reef diving and pleasant little villas and restaurants in the area, Amed is still the quietest resort area on Bali. Of course, with no real tourist centre, ATMs, or even a post office, it's not really even a resort, simply a few modest villages – (from north to south) **Amed**, **Jemeluk**, **Bunutan**, **Lipah**, **Lehan**, **Selang**, **Banyuning** and **Aas** – set in small inlets running along roughly 10km (6 miles) of coastline. Fishing, salt production and a few dry crops have traditionally been the main focus, and even with the increasing number of small hotels,

The view from the highland at Amed's Jemeluk Bay

Mountain bikes are handy for exploring Bali's more remote areas

mountain-bike trips through the rural areas around Gunung Batur in the northeast, and Gunung Batukaru, northwest of Ubud. On a bike you can travel through parts of the tranquil countryside that would be inaccessible by car or motorbike, taking trails through rice paddies and rainforests, and see first-hand some of the traditional ways of life as practised by the rural Balinese for centuries. Bali Sobek also offers free transfers from your hotel in Ubud or any of the southern resort areas. If there are other parts of Bali you'd prefer to see, the company can also design a customised tour; just give them at least two days' advance notice.

cafés and dive operators opening up in the area, the refreshingly authentic feel of Amed offers a pleasing contrast to the comfortable but overdeveloped atmosphere of most of the other tourist areas. The headland at Jemeluk Bay offers a sweeping view up the coast, with neat rows of fishing boats laid out along the black-sand beaches ready for the next expedition, and in salt-production season you'll see long, hollowed-out tree trunks laid out in the sun for the evaporation process. Most of the area's facilities are found in the central villages of Jemeluk, Bunutan and Lipah, but everything here is very spread out, so you'll need to use *bemos* or *ojeks*, or your own transport.

Biking through rural Bali

If you're short on time but still want to get away from it all for even a day, Bali Sobek (*see p166*) offers full-day, guided

Gunung Batukaru Eco-Lodge

The Sarinbuana Eco-Lodge is a nature lover's dream. Set in the largest rainforest on Bali, 750m (2,460ft) up the slope of Gunung Batukaru (*see p68*), the lodge follows environmentally and socially responsible policies and has raised money for a local preservation project to have 18sq km (7sq miles) of the Sarinbuana rainforest officially declared a 'no-take' zone, with no harvesting, hunting, trapping or cutting down trees allowed within the boundaries. The lodge offers a variety of eco-themed activities: guided walks through the rainforest, full-day or overnight treks up Gunung Batukaru, environmental education programmes and weekend camps for schoolchildren, and a 20m (66ft) tall Eco Tower offering views of

The rainforests of Bali have beautiful waterfalls

South Bali and the mountains of Java and Lombok. There are also two bungalows for accommodation and an open-air restaurant serving breakfast, lunch and dinner.

Sarinbuana Eco-Lodge, Gunung Batukaru, Tabanan. Tel: (0361) 743 5198. www.baliecolodge.com

Nusa Penida

Just east of Nusa Lembongan island and many times larger, Nusa Penida consists of a hilly limestone karst plateau with spectacular cliffs along the southern coast and some villages and beaches along the northern coast. Tourism hasn't yet taken off here as it

has on Nusa Lembongan, English is hardly spoken, and it's a great place to escape the crowds. The island is best explored by motorbike or car, and you can follow the steep and narrow roads around the island for great views.

Nusa Penida has a bad reputation as the home of evil, and is generally avoided by the Balinese. Near Toyapakeh, in Sampalan, the eerie **Pura Dalem Penataran Ped** temple is where pilgrims come to appease the evil spirit I Macaling. It's worth visiting the Pura Dalem temple before moving on to Toyapakeh, 10km (6 miles) to the west, where there's a fine beach with views over to Nusa Lembongan and Bali. Other specific sights to catch include Bukit Mundi, the island's highest point at 529m (1,736ft), the dramatic limestone cliffs near Sebuluh, and the impressive temples of Pura Songaya and Pura Puseh Yehulaten near Sewana and Pura Batu Kuning near Semaya. Boats to Nusa Penida are available at Padang Bai.

Seminyak and further north

Bali's many Western expats long ago fled the frenetic commercialism of Kuta and headed north to nearby Seminyak, making it the more restrained and stylish area it is today. For even less-peopled areas, head up to the coastal villages further north: **Kerobokan, Berewa** (or Brawa), **Canggu** and **Pantai Pererenan**. Just 10km (6 miles) north of the dense Kuta streets you'll find a placid rural area dotted with small hotels and rental villas set amid rice paddies, and rugged coastlines of near-deserted beaches with crashing surf and a refreshing lack of hawkers. (The currents and rips can be quite strong – beginner surfers should stick to Kuta beach – and there are no lifeguards, so hotels encourage their guests to use their pools for swimming instead.)

You'll need your own transport or taxis if you want to get to and fro around here, although some hotels offer free shuttle services to Seminyak or other nearby areas. Most of the facilities in these areas are slightly inland, placed along the roads that turn off from the main thoroughfare (the continued

extension of Jalan Raya Seminak) and run down to the beaches, next to which you'll find a smattering of local *warung* catering to the die-hard surfers who like to beat the crowds at Canggu, Berewa and Pantai Pererenan. Jalan Raya Kerobokan is also notable for being home to some of the best restaurants on Bali.

Taman Nasional Bali Barat (West Bali National Park)

Most of the far west of Bali comprises the 760sq km (294sq miles) of the island's only national park, which has pristine natural areas of forested mountains and coastal savannahs

The quieter beaches of Bali offer a chance for solitude

abounding in native flora and fauna. There are more than 200 species of plants and 160 different bird species, including one of the few found only on Bali: the beautiful and very rare Bali starling (*leucopsar Rothschildi*), a white bird with bright blue eye-patches and black-tipped wings, of which there are thought to be perhaps fewer than a dozen left in the wild. The park has a conservation centre which you can visit by purchasing a permit. There are also several different kinds of monkeys, deer, pigs, buffalo, lizards and snakes. The last Bali tiger was spotted in 1937, by a Dutch official who promptly shot it. There are a number of birdwatching walks and hiking trails of varying lengths and exertion levels, but all visitors must be accompanied by an authorised guide, which you can arrange at the park headquarters. The park's coastal areas also offer boat trips and diving and snorkelling at sites like the spectacular Pulau Menjangan (*see pp90–91*).

Taman Nasional Bali Barat Headquarters, Cekik (3km/2 miles south of Gilimanuk). Tel: (0365) 610 60. Office open: Mon–Thur 8am–3.30pm, Fri 8am–11am. Guides are available outside of office hours. Admission charge.

LOMBOK

In a way, all of Lombok is a good place to get away from mass tourism, but some special quiet spots are recommended for adventurous travellers who really want to escape.

High-walled rice paddy terraces in Sapit

The deserted lagoon at Sira, on Lombok

Sapit

A few minutes' drive away from the pass road towards Sembalun Lawang, Sapit is beautifully situated amid the foothills of Gunung Rinjani, and boasts excellent views across the high-walled rice-paddy terraces towards Sumbawa, the next large island. Agriculture is still done the traditional way, and plenty of villagers and farm animals can be seen working the fields.

Sira beach

Also known as Sire beach, this strip of white sand fringed by coconut trees can be reached by following the road to the nearby Kosaido golf course. The adjacent bay is clean, shallow and calm, and great for children and snorkelling. There are no facilities or distractions at all, apart from plantation workers who will offer to crack open a fresh coconut for you. And it's perfectly feasible as a day trip from Senggigi.

Southwest peninsula

The small road south of Lembar twists and turns from bay to bay with views over the scattering of islands as it proceeds west along the coast of the southwest peninsula. Find a beautiful pristine beach to call yours for the day, or charter a boat in Lembar or Tawun and cross over to the enchanting islands of Gili Nanggu, Gili Sudak or Gili Tangkong, which have more excellent beaches and diving. Far from the crowds on Bali and the more popular Gili Islands to the north, this is where you'll find true peace.

When to go

One of Bali's biggest draws is its climate – what's a tropical paradise without hot, sunny weather? The island's equatorial location gives it fairly constant temperatures, and nights are cooler but still warm enough for short sleeves and light clothing. The two natural seasons are rainy and dry, but much more likely to have an impact on your trip are the three tourist seasons: low, high and peak (when bookings can go a year in advance).

Climate

Only 8 degrees south of the equator, temperatures on the islands are warm and constant year-round, averaging 27°C (81°F) on the coasts during the day and slightly cooler, but still quite comfortable, at night. In the higher inland regions, temperatures are cooler still, averaging around 22°C (72°F) during the day and slightly cooler at night. A light jacket will be good to have in these areas if you're staying overnight.

Balinese women regularly use head-baskets to transport their goods

The two main seasons are dry (April to October) and rainy (November to March), with the wettest months being December and January. Don't assume that the rainy season is an unsuitable time for a visit; although tropical rains are notoriously unpredictable and quite heavy, they generally fall for only an hour or two, usually in the afternoon. Everyone scurries inside for a bit, but then the sun comes out again and the streets return to life. Overnight downpours can also occur, but offer the chance to fall asleep to the soothing sounds of rain on the roof. Packing a light poncho or travel umbrella is a good idea if you visit during these months. Due to muddy roads and trails, mountain climbing is not recommended during the rainy season. Be aware that the Ubud and Tabanan areas, both major rice-growing regions, can get rain at any time of the year.

Humidity is a constant, usually around 75 per cent in the dry season, and sometimes as high as 90 per cent in the wet months, so look for rooms with air conditioning if you find humidity uncomfortable.

Tourist seasons

More significant than the natural seasons are the tourist ones. High season is generally during the dry months of June to September (the northern hemisphere's summer holiday period), and sometimes includes Easter and Chinese New Year (early February). Peak season, which sees the biggest crowds and the highest prices, is December to January, coinciding with the Christmas and New Year holidays. Hotels in these periods will be more expensive and booked out far in advance, so plan ahead. If you visit during the remaining months (low season), however, you'll find things much quieter, with fewer tourists and often greatly discounted prices on hotels, goods and services.

Lombok

Lombok's high seasons coincide with those of Bali, with peaks from Christmas to late January and from June to September. It's wise to book your hotel in advance during these months. Even then, the number of tourists visiting Lombok is much less than the masses descending on Bali, and it is still quite easy to escape the crowds away from the main tourist destinations. Outside peak seasons, even Senggigi and the Gili Islands can seem completely deserted and great

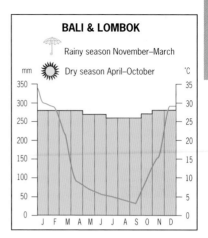

BALI & LOMBOK

Rainy season November–March

Dry season April–October

WEATHER CONVERSION CHART

25.4mm = 1 inch

°F = 1.8 × °C + 32

deals can be had on accommodation prices. Unless you have a specific hotel in mind, there's no need to book ahead; simply shop around for the nicest room on arrival.

THE HARD SELL

You'll get constant offerings of goods and transport at any time of the year, especially around Kuta and other tourist areas. In low-season months business is slow and there are fewer tourists to ask, so the offers may seem unrelenting. Don't get annoyed or lose your temper; remember, they're just trying to earn a living. A polite 'No, thank you' as you continue walking away is the best way to handle it; don't say 'Maybe later' unless you mean it, as they *will* remember you. And don't start bargaining unless you're interested; if they accept your offer, you're obligated to buy.

Getting around

Both Bali and Lombok are small enough to drive across in a few hours (from the south of Bali to the north takes approximately 3 hours), which makes it relatively easy to cover a lot of ground. However, road quality, traffic and public transport can cause a lot of headaches, and there are no rail services on either island. Your best bets for a hassle-free trip are taxis in the southern tourist areas around Kuta and Denpasar, and tourist shuttles or private drivers for countryside sightseeing or trips to other towns.

Public transport

Bemos (minivans)

Brightly coloured minivans called *bemos* are the most common form of public transport. They have set routes (but no timetables) and can be caught at a terminal in larger towns or flagged down along the road. Fares are paid directly to the driver upon disembarking; passengers simply yell 'Stop!' when they want to get off. Although fares are fixed, in reality tourists will be asked for several times what the locals pay, and many drivers won't let you on until this has been negotiated. Be sure that you have plenty of small notes or coins with you (Rp10,000 and under), as drivers won't be able to give change for large notes. Although cheap and ubiquitous, *bemos* can be slow and uncomfortable, and are not recommended for long trips with luggage. Beware of pickpockets when stuck in traffic jams.

Motorbike touts

Known as *ojek*, these drivers of motorbikes or scooters take paying passengers riding pillion. They are more commonly used in smaller or more spread-out resort areas, but are seen everywhere.

Taxis

Metered taxis are a fast, convenient and inexpensive way to get around the sprawling areas near Kuta and Denpasar, and your best option if you're going to or from Nusa Dua or travelling around Mataram and Senggigi on Lombok. Look for the light-blue **Bali Blue Bird Taxis** (*Tel: (0361) 701 111*) or Lombok's **Blue Bird Taxis** (*Tel: (0370) 627 000*), both reliable companies with air-conditioned cars and English-speaking drivers. Just flag one down and hop in, and make sure the meter is on. General practice when paying is to round up to the nearest Rp1,000.

A Balinese family taking in the view on Jimbaran

Tourist shuttles
Perama (*Tel: (0361) 751 551.
www.peramatour.com*), one of the best-
established private transport
companies, runs daily shuttle buses
between Kuta (and the airport), Sanur,
Ubud, Lovina, Padang Bai and Candi
Dasa. Although more expensive than
bemos, they're faster, more comfortable,
have room for luggage and offer fixed
timetables, and hotel pick-ups and
drop-offs are even available for a small
fee. Phone or enquire at hotels or the
local Perama office for bookings (one
day in advance is recommended).
The company also offers boats to
Lombok and the Gili Islands (*see p131*).
Sample fares from Kuta (at the time of
writing) are as follows: Sanur,
Rp25,000; Ubud, Rp50,000; Padang
Bai/Candi Dasa, Rp60,000; Lovina,
Rp125,000.

Private transport
Bicycles
Bikes are available in most tourist
centres for around Rp25,000 per day.
In Ubud, a bike is good for touring the
countryside, but inspect it carefully first
and take plenty of water and sun
protection. Guided, full-day mountain
bike tours are also available (*see p166*);
you'll pay more but will have the
security of not getting lost or worrying
about the equipment.

Cars
Driving around Bali requires an
international driving licence and nerves
of steel. Traffic is chaotic (at best),

streets narrow and confusingly laid out, and roads often poorly maintained and lacking clear signage. Police also regularly stop foreigners for on-the-spot 'fines' (see p159). Prices for a local vehicle (look for rental signs) are around Rp100,000 per day in low season. Be sure to ask about insurance and inspect the vehicle carefully first. Traffic drives on the left. For an island-wide driving map, try the Periplus *Street Atlas Bali*.

Driver with vehicle

Chartering a driver with his own car lets you sightsee according to your own itinerary without having to worry about navigating Bali's tricky roads. A full day's hire will cost around Rp300,000–400,000, including fuel. (It's courteous to buy your driver lunch if you're out all day.) Finding one is easy; ask at your hotel or talk to the men on the street who call out 'Transport!' as you walk by. Ask what they drive (usually a jeep or small minivan),

whether it's air conditioned, and be prepared to negotiate. You can also ring **Wayan** in Kuta (*Tel: (0812) 396 1296*), **Putu** in Ubud (*Tel: (081) 338 741 541*) or **Gede** in Lovina (*Tel: (0812) 398 2941*).

Horse carts

Called *dokar* on Bali, they're a tourist staple around the Kuta area – just listen for the harness bells. Negotiate a fare before getting in, but don't expect to pay less than Rp10,000 for even a short ride. On Lombok, they're called *cidomos* and are used mostly for taking villagers and their goods to market. On the Gili Islands, these are the only vehicles apart from bicycles.

Motorcycles and scooters

Most of the same advice applies as for cars. In more remote areas motorbikes can be convenient, but only for experienced drivers with an international motorcycle driving licence. Helmets are required and

Perama's tourist boat, ready for the trip from Padang Bai to Lombok

accidents are common, so take special care. You'll find fuel sold from bottles at roadside stands. Prices are around Rp50,000 per day for a scooter.

Lombok

Lombok is easily reached from Bali. Local airlines, including Merpati and Transnusa, fly to Mataram's airport several times per day. The 20-minute flight costs about Rp300,000 one-way and offers fine views of Gunung Agung and Nusa Penida.

The Perama bus from Kuta and Ubud connects to their 1.30pm tourist boat service from Padang Bai directly to the Gili Islands (5 hours, Rp200,000 including meal). The return trip is from Senggigi; a shuttle boat from the Gilis to Bangsal on the mainland departs at about 7am and a connecting minibus takes you to Senggigi in time for the 9am departure to Padang Bai.
Gilicat (*Tel: (0361) 271 680. www.gilicat.com*) offers fast, 80-minute boat transfers between Bali and Lombok, departing daily from Sanur at 9am to Gili Trawangan and Teluk Kode (south of Bangsal); return is at 11.30am and extra departures are added when demand is high. Costs are Rp660,000 one way or Rp1,200,000 return, including transfers from Kuta, Seminyak and Legian.
BlueWater Express (*Tel: (0361) 3104 558. www.bwsbali.com*) has a daily fast boat at 8am from Benoa marina (near Kuta) to Gili Trawangan and Teluk Kode in $2^1/_2$ hours; return is at 11.30am.

There are also regular ferries between Padang Bai and Lembar every 90 minutes, taking 4–6 hours depending on if the dock at Lembar is occupied on arrival. If you're travelling without your own transportation, it's wise to book onward travel from Lembar in advance (with Perama, for instance), as the *bemo* touts there show no mercy to unprepared tourists. It's possible to take rental cars and motorbikes from Bali to Lombok, but check this carefully with the rental agency first.

Lombok's Blue Bird taxis (*see p128*) are your best bet for short trips. Driving on Lombok is more pleasant as there's much less traffic. Car rental is available at the airport, but is much cheaper at the travel agents in Senggigi. Prices are similar to or slightly higher than those on Bali. It's wise to get a copy of the Periplus *Travelmap Lombok & Sumbawa*, which is the only good road map of the island. Unfortunately, it is not available anywhere on Lombok and you'll have to buy it at Bali's airport or Kuta's bookshops.

Perama runs daily buses from Senggigi to Lombok's main tourist destinations including Mataram/Cakranegara, Tetebatu and Kuta. *Bemos* on Lombok are very cheap and useful for short hops on Lombok, but are uncomfortable and slow for longer trips. Tourists using *bemos* are more of a rarity here and you won't be cheated as often as on Bali.

Accommodation

Accommodation on Bali truly runs the gamut from A to Z. Whether you want a cold-water room with a ceiling fan for only a few dollars per night or a luxury suite with hundred-count cotton sheets and a marble bathtub for two, you can find it here. Nusa Dua is home to the biggest resorts, but lovely mid-range hotels can also be found in other areas. The ubiquitous losmen *(guesthouses) offer basic comfort at the best value.*

Top-end

If you're looking to splurge, try Nusa Dua and Tanjung Benoa in the south. Some of the world's finest resort hotels can be found here – often charging only as much as a mid-range hotel in New York or London – and you can expect everything about the décor, food and service to be top-notch. Besides the gorgeous swimming pools and white-sand beaches, you'll also find health and fitness clubs, massage and beauty spas, a full calendar of sporting and social activities, and children's clubs to amuse the little ones while you relax. Nearby are shopping plazas and golf clubs, and day trips to cultural sights can be arranged. Anything you could want will be provided on-site, but keep in mind that these super-scrubbed areas have been custom-built for tourists, so while it can be an appealing haven for lounging by the pool while sipping cool drinks and getting a massage, you won't be seeing anything resembling 'the real Bali' unless you take the time to travel to other parts of the island.

Mid-range

Lovely mid-range hotels can be found in all the major tourist centres, as well as dotted around the smaller ones. These will sometimes offer a broad price-range of rooms with differing décor and amenities, so you can save a bit of money if you're happy to forgo some luxury. Western-style toilets and air conditioning are standard, and amenities sometimes include satellite TVs and minibars. Bathrooms are often 'garden style', planted with lush green foliage and featuring an open half-roof to let you shower under the stars – a nod to the Balinese custom of bathing outdoors. (Fear not; you still have full privacy.)

Individual rooms in high-rise hotels are uncommon here. Most hotels will offer separate or semi-detached cottages for accommodation, and some even have full Balinese-style bungalows, including ornately carved double doors, traditional art and décor, and traditional wooden furniture, such as four-poster beds with muslin mosquito netting. A modest breakfast (a choice of eggs and toast or banana pancakes and fruit, for example) is usually included in the price of the room. While lacking in the full-service features of the big resorts, these hotels have swimming pools and a restaurant, and most will be able to arrange transportation or tourist and cultural activities on request.

Low-end

On the lower end of the scale, more modest – and money-saving – accommodation can be found everywhere in *losmen* ('guesthouses'), Bali's equivalent of budget hotels or hostels. Rooms are very simply decorated, sometimes with older, unmatched furniture, air conditioning is often available only in the higher-end rooms (although a ceiling fan can keep a room quite cool at night), and while a small fridge is sometimes provided, it's doubtful you'll get a television or phone. (The cheapest rooms don't always have hot water, so ask before booking.) However, you can usually expect friendly and personalised service from the staff, who might make you feel like part of the family, especially in low season. Breakfast is also included, and most *losmen* also have a swimming pool and restaurant, so you may be surprised at how much you actually get for quite a low price.

Shower under the stars in a garden-style bathroom

Palace stays

For a regal twist, try a guestroom in one of Bali's royal palaces, such as Central Bali's Puri Anyar (Krambitan) or Puri Saren Agung (Ubud). Banquet dinners, traditional dances and cultural lessons can be arranged by your hosts, members of some of Bali's oldest royal families. Advanced bookings are required (*see listings, pp164 & 166*).

Booking

If you're not using a travel agent, you can either book online at the hotel's site or *www.indo.com*, or contact the hotel directly by email, phone or fax. For high or peak season, you'll definitely need to book well in advance; during low season, you may be able to find some good deals after arrival, by

Beachfront hut on Gili Air, Lombok

negotiating in person (if you don't mind lugging your bags around in search of discounts). Taxes and service charges are generally not included in published rates, so always enquire about extra costs (usually called 'plus-plus', meaning tax plus service) before booking.

Lombok

Accommodation on Lombok is not as developed as on Bali, but most visitors think that's a good thing. There are a dozen top-end resort hotels spread over the island, but they're not as large and isolated from local life as those on Bali. The service may be more relaxed than on Bali, but prices can be much lower too and, especially in low season, you can stay at a dream resort for a bargain.

The beachside resort hotels can be found in Kuta, Senggigi, Gili Trawangan and along the north coast. Gili Trawangan also has a number of luxury villas for rent, which can often be booked through the dive centres. Mataram has only two upmarket hotels, as most tourists head straight for Senggigi. Lombok's tourist guesthouses (*pondok*) are usually quite basic but clean and excellent value for money. It's wise to view a few options before checking in somewhere, as standards can vary a lot.

On the Gili Islands there are dozens of guesthouses along the beaches, most of them offering accommodation in simple, fan-cooled bamboo stilt huts with verandahs and attached concrete bathrooms. Prices are cheap but can vary greatly between high and low seasons. Note that breakfast is often included in the price at guesthouses, but could be limited to just a pancake or omelette.

Luxurious cabins on Lombok

Sustainable travel

Bali and Lombok are small islands and the tourism industry greatly affects natural resources and residents' lives. Below are some suggestions on travelling responsibly. For more ideas, consult Ethical Traveler (*www.ethicaltraveler.org*) or Baliblog (*www.baliblog.com/travel-tips/responsible-tourism-in-bali.html*).

Recently, deforestation due to demand for wood and water shortage problems has become so severe that the new governor of Bali is taking the first steps to limit exploitation of underground water sources, replant forests and limit development in crowded areas to protect Bali's nature and culture.

The downside of tourism

- Cut down on your waste and reuse or recycle things where you can. The enormous scale of tourism can overwhelm waste management systems and rubbish has become a real problem. Refill your plastic water bottle instead of buying new ones; some restaurants sell spring water for refilling (do not drink the tap water).
- Remember that Western travellers are incredibly rich by local standards. Avoid gratuitous displays of wealth, and be generous when haggling for prices – the equivalent of a few coins for you is worth far more for them.
- Respect cultural traditions by observing appropriate dress codes, especially at temples and holy sites. Avoid revealing clothing or vulgar behaviour that could offend local sensibilities.
- Consider the environmental impact of your activities. Opt for eco-friendlier options like public transport, bicycles or walking when you can. Keep golf course visits to a miniumum.
- Reduce electricity use by turning off (or down) your lights and air conditioning when leaving your hotel room.

Many artists and craftspeople sell their goods themselves

- Use water resources wisely. Take showers instead of baths and ask cleaning staff to not replace your towels and linens daily. The islands depend on water for agriculture – rice is especially water-intensive – and hotels and restaurants use thousands of litres per day.
- Don't buy items produced from endangered animals or plants, such as turtles, ivory or coral. Indonesian law also forbids exporting these items.
- Coral reefs are very fragile. If you go diving or snorkelling, take care not to step on them or remove any pieces.
- Treat local people with respect. Don't get angry over small matters like slow service. Always ask before taking photos of people or their homes. Have conversations with them to learn about their lives. Buy a phrase book and learn some basic phrases – you'll be amazed at how warmly your linguistic efforts will be received.
- Support the local economy. Buy from Balinese merchants wherever possible. Eat in local restaurants instead of international chains. Buy locally produced arts and crafts – especially from the artisans themselves – instead of shopping at foreign-owned stores. Hire local guides instead of package tour companies. Spread your spending power over a variety of shops and services instead of repeatedly using the same ones.
- Giving cash or gifts to children can encourage them to become beggars. Donating money or needed items to a local charity or school will help more in the long run.
- Consider donating money or volunteering your time to an organisation dedicated to improving conditions on Bali and Lombok. There are numerous non-profits and NGOs in the area that need your help for work with environmental and wildlife conservation (*www.gus-bali.org*, *www.globalcoral.org*, *www.fnpf.org*), poverty (*www.eastbalipovertyproject.org*), sustainable living (*www.idepfoundation.org*), education (*www.balihati.org*, *www.rolefoundation.org*), fair trade (*www.mitrabali.com*) and medical care (*www.balicrisiscare.org*).

Food and drink

Unlike other destinations, it's not easy to find true Balinese food on Bali. Most of the food eaten by locals is actually Indonesian or Chinese in origin, although some Balinese dishes can be found on menus, and there are a few restaurants devoted entirely to the cuisine. Tourism brought about a huge surge in global restaurants, and you can find everything from sushi to tapas, pizzas to paella, and beef burritos to chicken tikka, at a wide range of prices to suit any budget.

In most tourist areas, you'll find restaurants either devoted to one cuisine (e.g. Thai, Japanese, Mexican, etc.), or with a wide-ranging menu featuring Indonesian and Chinese dishes alongside Western foods like pizza, pastas, burgers and grilled steaks, chicken or fish. At the cheaper restaurants you may need to adjust your expectations for the latter – pizza and burgers are not native dishes, after all. Consult *www.balieats.com* for a comprehensive database of restaurant reviews, searchable by cuisine and location.

For a more authentic experience, head for a local warung (café). They range greatly in size and prices, but will generally feature a menu of Indonesian (and sometimes Balinese) dishes of meat, poultry or fish with vegetables, accompanied by rice (nasi) or noodles (mie). Pork (babi), chicken (ayam), fish (ikan) and prawns (udang) are the most common options, but vegetarians will rejoice at the frequency of dishes with tofu (tahu) and tempeh.

Common favourites include *nasi goreng* (chicken or seafood with fried rice) and *mie goreng* (with fried noodles), *gado-gado* (tofu and vegetables with spicy peanut sauce and prawn crackers) and various kinds of *saté* (skewers of grilled meat, usually served with peanut sauce). Particularly

Grilling up some *saté* on the streets of Kuta

Local sweets for sale at a Denpasar market stall

good is the *nasi campur* ('cham-poor'), a cone of rice surrounded by small portions of different meats, fish and vegetables, often including tofu, prawn crackers and a spicy condiment called *sambal*. (Vegetarian versions are commonly available.)

For non-alcoholic drinks, try a deliciously thirst-quenching *lassi* (a yoghurt smoothie with tropical fruit). Alcoholic options include imported wine (often from Australia), beer (Bintang is the favourite local choice) and *arak*, a potent rice wine usually mixed with lemon and honey.

Balinese dishes

Two authentic Balinese dishes commonly advertised are *babi guling* (spit-roasted suckling pig) and *bebek betutu* (marinated duck steamed in banana leaves). However, both generally require ordering a day in advance, so look for signs and plan ahead.

Taxes and tipping

Higher-end restaurants will usually include a 10 per cent service charge in the bill; smaller places generally won't, but tips are always appreciated for good service. Round bills up to the nearest Rp1,000 when paying.

Lombok

Lombok's Sasak people, some 90 per cent of the population, are mostly Muslims so you won't find as much pork served here but, more so than on Bali, there is a distinct local cuisine here. Sasak food makes use of rice, vegetables, meat and plenty of hot red Lombok peppers to spice things up. Look for signature dishes such as *ayam taliwang* (chicken in hot chilli sauce), *gule lemak* (beef curry) and *sayur nangka* (jackfruit curry). At markets, look for ladies selling *plosor*, a delicious sweet snack consisting of rice cake, honey, palm oil and coconut, served on a banana leaf.

Entertainment

Traditional culture is one of Bali's biggest draws as a destination, and performances of Balinese dances accompanied by gamelan music are available in every tourist area, although Ubud has the finest troupes and the best choice of shows. The other main entertainment options are bars (often with live music) and nightclubs, the hippest of which are found in Kuta, Legian and Seminyak. Of course, on a tropical island, spending a warm night on the beach is always a popular option, too.

Cultural performances

Ubud is the best place to experience traditional dances accompanied by gamelan orchestras, with at least four or five shows every night of the week staged in various venues around the area (free transport is available for the furthest sites). Popular choices include the lively kecak (monkey) and barong (lion) dances, and the graceful female

A gamelan musician about to strike

legong dancers. Some shows present a medley of styles. Try to see whatever's playing at the Ubud Palace; the beautiful surroundings greatly enhance the show. Current schedules are available from the tourist information kiosk on Jalan Raya Ubud or from *www.whatsupbali.com/dance.* Shows start at 7–8pm and last around 60–90 minutes. General-seating tickets cost around Rp8,000 and are available from the tourist office, touts or at the door. If you can't make it to Ubud, dances are also held frequently in Denpasar, Batubulan, and in select hotels and restaurants in other tourist centres of Bali. Enquire at your hotel for details. For current entertainment listings, pick up a copy of *The Beat* magazine or check the websites *www.beatmag.com* and *www.whatsupbali.com*

Nightlife

The Kuta/Legian area has a seemingly infinite number of pubs, bars and nightclubs, located mostly along Jalan

Legian, Jalan Pantai Kuta and the larger cross-streets. Bars and clubs here can go on until 3–4am, attracting young Westerners (especially Australians) and Indonesians looking to drink cheaply and party heartily. DJs spin anything from reggae to house music, and many places regularly feature live music.

Further north in Seminyak, especially along Jalan Dhyana Pura, are more chilled-out bars and sophisticated nightclubs with hot cocktails and cool beats, often frequented by expats avoiding the tourist throngs of Kuta. If you want to dress up and dance till dawn, they're a good bet on weekends. Nusa Dua hasn't any real nightlife beyond the few clubs and bars some of the luxury resorts make available for their guests.

Sanur and Ubud both have some low-key bars with live music, mostly reggae, jazz or Latin, but they close by midnight or 1am (Ubud's by-laws prohibit nightclubs entirely). Lovina has a weekend disco in Banyualit (*see p170*) that attracts a local crowd and some tourists, but the area's low-key vibe is best experienced in the relaxed bars on Jalan Bina Ria in Kalibukbuk, where a few feature regular live music (with muted football matches on in the background), and close around 1 or 2am.

Lombok

Traditional entertainment on Lombok is limited to performances during religious festivals, and occasional dance shows held at the larger hotels. The island has several unique dances, including the *batek baris* dance, which imitates Dutch soldiers marching around. Nightlife is restricted to the handful of lively bars and clubs in Senggigi and Gili Trawangan.

Cockfights

Cockfights are popular on both islands, and you'll often see baskets holding cherished roosters waiting for battle. Cockfighting is officially banned in Indonesia as a form of gambling, but is permitted for religious purposes, so fights are often held on temple grounds (with the frenetic betting clearly just a 'coincidence'). If you can stand the gore and are interested in attending one, just ask around.

You don't have to be an Aussie to like an all-night Happy Hour

Shopping

Serious shoppers will swoon at the amazing range, quality and value of goods available on Bali, but anyone would be hard-pressed to leave without buying at least a few trinkets. The Kuta and Ubud areas are both crammed with endless stores and pasar seni *(art markets) carrying all manner of goods and handicrafts: sarongs, baskets, shoes, T-shirts, paintings, ceramics, jewellery, woodcarvings and more. Of course, on Bali, you don't even need to hit the shops – they hit you.*

Certain towns are famous for particular craft specialities (see p56), and while you can find their goods for sale all over Bali, you may get better deals directly from the artisans. Just keep in mind that many of your purchases will require bargaining. Be prepared to deal with hawkers on most beaches and main streets (*see box, p127*).

If you're after general merchandise (books, clothes, gifts, electronics, etc.) and want convenience and fixed prices, the **Matahari Department Store** (*Jl Legian; Kuta Square*) is a good one-stop destination. For everyday, hassle-free food shopping, try **Bintang Supermarket** (*Jl Raya Seminyak; Jl Raya Campuhan (Ubud area); other locations*).

Antiques

It's against Indonesian law to export items more than 50 years old, so many 'antiques' may be reproductions of classic pieces. Check carefully for rot and enquire about shipping options before purchasing large items. If doing

the Denpasar Walk (*see pp34–5*), consider stopping in at **Arts of Asia** (*Jl Thamrin 27–37 Block C5. Tel: (0361) 423 350*), just a few blocks from the Kumbasari market. It has a remarkable collection of antiques, textiles, jewellery

Major international brands also have outlets in Bali

All sorts of crafts can be found at a *pasar seni* (art market)

and artefacts from all over Asia. Antique shops can also be found on the main streets of Singaraja in the north and Klungkung in the east.

Clothing and textiles

Whether it's traditional or cutting-edge, you can find it here. **Kuta Square** and Nusa Dua's **Bali Collection** shopping centre are lined with top Western stores, but there are also plenty of local brands you can show off at home. The trendy **Body & Soul** has a number of outlets in the Kuta area and Nusa Dua, and **Uluwatu** (in Kuta, Sanur and Ubud) is well known for its handmade lace clothing and home linens. Stores with sarongs and other Balinese styles can be found everywhere, especially

along Jalan Legian in Kuta or at any art market. Bali is also known for its traditional hand-woven textiles, including the intricate ikat, the finest examples of which can be found in the eastern village of Tenganan (*see pp78–9*), and the gold-and-silver brocade cloth *songket*, used for the exquisite *legong* costumes. **Threads of Life** (*Jl Kajeng 24, Ubud. Tel: (0361) 972 187. www.threadsoflife.com*) offers educational workshops in Indonesian weaving styles. Jalan Sulawesi in Denpasar (*see p35*) is the city's main textile street, and **Nogo Ikat Center** (*Jl Danau Tamblingan 104, Sanur. Tel: (0361) 288 765. www.nogobali.com. Open: 9am–9pm*) in Sanur sells all manner of items in traditional fabrics.

Handicrafts

The 'craft corridor' of towns between Denpasar and Ubud (*see p56*) is the source of most of the handicrafts you'll see for sale in Kuta, Ubud and everywhere else: Celuk for silverwork, Mas for woodcarvings, Batubulan for stone sculptures, Bedulu for terracotta pieces, Sukawati for the *wayang kulit* shadow puppets (also home to a large art market on the main road) and Batuan for its eponymous school of painting.

Jewellery

Celuk is the home of the famed Balinese silversmiths. Their work is sold everywhere, but in Celuk you can get custom pieces made to order. Try **Ketut Sunaka** (*Jl Jagaraga 28, Celuk. Tel: (0361) 298 275*), or **Yusuf Silver** (*Jl Legian 182. Tel: (0361) 752 050.*

Jalan Sulawesi is known for its textile stores

www.yusufsilver.com) in Kuta. Gold jewellery shops can be found on Jalan Hasanudin in Denpasar.

Paintings

Ubud is the home of Balinese painting, and its streets are lined with more art stores, galleries and museums than you can shake a paintbrush at (*see pp57–63*). Don't be surprised to find the same subjects or styles repeated everywhere, as perfect replication is considered a display of artistic skill. Ask about lower prices on unframed works for easier shipping home.

Lombok

Shopping on Lombok is limited but delightfully varied. There are tourist art markets in Senggigi and on Gili Trawangan, where you'll find a few fixed-price shops (ideal for checking out prices if you plan to bargain for an item elsewhere) as well as regular stalls selling crafts. Then there are the handicraft centres around Mataram (*see p104*) and Tetebatu (*see 'Drive: Tetebatu and the crafts villages', pp118–19*), where you can visit villages to browse shops for local crafts such as Lombok pottery, masks, woodcarvings, furniture, woven cloth and rattan products. Any taxi driver will know where to find the clutch of small antique shops beside the Jalan Yos Sudarso bridge in Ampenan, the harbour town attached to Mataram. Foldable, X-shaped wooden book holders, used for reading the Koran, are quite cheap, and there are plenty of other bargains. Pearls are a Lombok speciality, and the best range and prices are to be found at the dozen shops in the MCC Centre in Pagesangan, a short taxi ride south of Mataram. Of these, **Mutiara Global** (*Tel: (0370) 630 781. www.mutiaraglobal.com*) has the largest selection. The only mall on Lombok, the Mataram Mall in Cakranegara, has a useful supermarket and several adventure sports and surf shops as well as the usual international fast-food restaurants.

Traditional Lombok pottery for sale along the road

Sport and leisure

On a sun-blessed tropical island, outdoor activities are the main draws, especially those involving mountains or the sea. Bali's coral reefs allow for some of the best surfing, diving and snorkelling in the world, and volcano hiking and rural biking and trekking offer stunning views. Or try white-water rafting, bungee jumping, golf or just a relaxing massage.

Adventure activities

Tour companies offer river rafting and kayaking, mountain biking, and rural treks around the Ubud area, with complete full- and half-day packages. Sanur and Tanjung Benoa have great water sports, or you can bungee jump at Legian.

Diving and snorkelling

Bali's coral reefs have magnificent wall dives, shipwrecks and marine life (*see*

Bali is a surfer's paradise

pp42–3). Out west, Pulau Menjangan is a top choice for both diving and snorkelling, while the east has the Amed area and a popular shipwreck site at Tulamben. PADI-certified dive operators (*see www.padi.com*) have courses and tours for all levels.

Golf

Bali has several golf courses set amid its lush green hills, including the only one in the world located inside a volcanic crater (in Bedugul), and a Greg Norman-designed course in Tabanan that offers gorgeous views of Pura Tanah Lot and the ocean.

Hiking

Climbing up Bali's mountains, especially the eastern volcanoes Gunung Agung and Gunung Batur, can be an amazing but strenuous experience, and climbers should be healthy and fit to attempt them. A licensed guide is required or recommended for most of the big hikes. Don't attempt any climbs during the rainy season as landslides can occur.

Spas and massage

Bali has the highest concentration of spas in Southeast Asia, and all are in the top resorts and upscale areas like Seminyak and Ubud. Want to play queen or king for a day? Try *mandi lulur*, a luxurious, full-body treatment favoured by old Javanese royalty, featuring massage, exfoliation with a fragrant paste of herbs and spices, a cooling yoghurt mask, and finally a warm bath filled with flowers.

Spectator sports

The western town of Negara is home to Bali's yearly traditional buffalo races, where the ungainly creatures get their chance at fleet-footed glory while spurred on by cart-riding jockeys. Contact the **Jembrana Tourist Office** (*Tel: (0365) 412 10*) for information. More conveniently, Lovina holds weekly buffalo races for tourists in Kaliasem; look for flyers or ask at your hotel.

Surfing

Bali has fantastic surfing for all levels. The best surf beaches are at Kuta, Bukit Badung and Nusa Lembongan (*see pp42–3*). Surf tour operators can take experienced enthusiasts to the more remote spots, and beginners will find schools and surf stores around Kuta.

Lombok

Diving, snorkelling and surfing are the most popular activities on Lombok. It's easiest to arrange diving courses and excursions from Senggigi and the Gili Islands, where most dive centres are based. Experienced divers should consider booking trips to Lombok's south coast, where the *mola mola* (ocean sunfish), the world's largest fish, can be spotted. Surfers rave about Lombok's breaks – the coasts around Kuta and especially Devil Point near Bangko Bangko (at the extreme southwestern tip of Lombok) offer world-class surfing. Hiking up Gunung Rinjani volcano is also very popular, and guided treks of two days up to a week can be arranged in Senggigi or Senaru. Less strenuous leisure options include golfing at Lombok's 18-hole courses, and soaking in a spa, which is possible at most resort hotels.

The golf course near Pemenang, Lombok

Children

Bali is a great destination for kids. Besides family fun at the beach, there are plenty of exciting activities and sights that children of all ages can enjoy. Most large resorts have babysitting services or children's clubs that offer activities and painting, dance and craft classes, and many have wading pools. The Balinese love children – and will probably make more of a fuss over yours than you do.

Activities

Bali Adventure Tours and Bali Sobek

These companies offer cycling, trekking and white-water rafting trips for families with children aged 7 and up (*see listings, p166*).

Bali Treetop Adventure Park

This new park, near the Botanical Gardens in Bedugul, features adventure circuits for all ages (with full safety harnesses), including rope bridges, flying-fox lines, rope swings and more. *Tel: (081) 338 306 898. www.balitreetop.com*

Scuba Duba Doo and Ripcurl School of Surf

These schools, like most scuba diving and surf schools in the Kuta area, offer courses specially tailored for children (*see listings, p162*).

The Balinese are all smiles around children

Waterbom Park

Just south of Kuta, this place offers a great way to beat the heat, with all kinds of watery rides and slides, leisure pools, a supervised area for under-12s, restaurants, a spa, and lifeguards on duty at all times.
Tel: (0361) 755 676. www.waterbom.com

Wildlife parks

Central Bali has some animal parks that will delight kids, such as the **Bali Bird & Reptile Parks** and the **Bali Zoo Park** (*see p56*) and the **Elephant Safari Park** (*see pp64–5*). Wild monkeys inhabit **Pura Luhur Uluwatu** (*see pp45–6*) and the **Monkey Forest Sanctuary** (*see pp59–60*), but the clever creatures have learned to snatch loose items (hats, eyeglasses, etc.) to exchange for food, so their antics may frighten very young children.

Lombok

Children are universally adored on Lombok, and although the tourism industry is perhaps less geared towards children than on Bali, there's no reason not to bring them along. Most resort hotels have pools with separate shallow areas for safe paddling. The beaches on the Gili Islands and around Kuta are shallow and don't have large waves, making them ideal for children, too. Children will love seeing the wild monkeys at Pusuk Pass, though be very careful when feeding them as they can be aggressive; it's best to watch from a distance or from inside the car. When visiting traditional villages, children can

A troop of grey macaques live at Pura Luhur Uluwatu

play with their Sasak counterparts and experience how these children live and what their school looks like.

Practical tips

- Enquire at hotels about family suites or self-contained bungalows.
- Restaurant staff are usually quite happy to mind young ones while you enjoy your meal.
- Streets are often bumpy, with high kerbs. Sport-style strollers or shoulder harnesses are best for transporting infants.
- Disposable nappies are available on Bali, but they're pricey. You're best to bring your own or use cloth ones.
- Take extra precautions to protect your children from the strong sun and heat.
- Larger families might find hiring a driver with a minivan easier than taking public transport or taxis.
- Avoid temporary tattoos. The dyes can be unsafe for sensitive skin.
- Try *www.baliforfamilies.com* and *www. balifamilyholidays.com* for more advice.

Essentials

Arriving

By air

Ngurah Rai Airport (abbreviated DPS, also called Denpasar), located 3km (2 miles) south of Kuta, handles all international and domestic flights for Bali, and is served by leading carriers from Europe, the USA, Australia and Asia. Quite modest compared to others in Asia, it offers facilities for 24-hour currency exchange, hotel reservations and car rentals, along with ATMs and some food and retail outlets.

Many hotels offer airport pick-up; ask when making your booking. Fixed-fare taxis to popular destinations are available. Pay at the counter in the Arrivals area and you'll receive a coupon to give to the driver. Metered taxis are cheaper but must be hailed on the street outside the airport gates – turn right out of Arrivals and walk about 500m (550 yds). Avoid any transport touts who approach you at the terminal.

Lombok's Selaparang Airport (AMI) is conveniently located 2km (1¼ miles) north of Mataram and 8km (5 miles) southeast of Senggigi, and can be reached from several Indonesian cities as well as from Singapore. There are ATMs and restaurants, as well as a fixed-fare taxi counter. However, it's cheaper to walk 100m (110 yds) from the terminal to the main road and hail one of the waiting Blue Bird taxis, which always use their meters and charge about 40 per cent less than the airport taxis.

By sea

If you'd prefer to sail to Lombok instead of fly, **Perama** (*www.peramatour.com*) and **Gilicat** (*www.gilicat.com*) offer a tourist boat service directly to the Gili Islands, leaving from Padang Bai (*see p131*).

Customs

Visitors are allowed to bring in the following items: 200 cigarettes, 50 cigars or 100g of tobacco, one litre of alcohol, perfume clearly for personal use, and up to 10 million Rupiah. Prohibited are narcotic and psychotropic drugs, weapons and ammunition, pornographic materials, and printed matter with Chinese characters. Pre-recorded videotapes and discs may be subject to censorship. Animals, fish and plants may be subject to quarantine.

Departing

Departure tax is payable in cash only: Rp150,000 (international) and Rp30,000 (domestic) from Bali, and Rp30,000 (domestic) from Lombok. Don't lose the Indonesian disembarkation card you filled out on arrival, as it is required on departure.

Electricity

Developed areas have all been upgraded to 230V/50Hz, but some of the most remote areas may still use 110V. Outlets take plugs with two round pins. 110V appliances will need a transformer. All tourist destinations on Bali and Lombok have reliable electricity.

Internet and email

Internet cafés are widely available in tourist centres, but speeds and prices can vary widely. Most tourist centres around Bali will offer moderate broadband at approximately Rp200–300 per minute; in more remote areas, you may get only dial-up at twice the price. Lombok has internet cafés charging around Rp500 per minute in the main tourist destinations, though the connections are extremely slow. Upmarket hotels can offer faster connections at around Rp1,000 per hour.

Money

Currency

Indonesia uses the Rupiah, abbreviated as Rp. Notes are available in denominations of 100,000, 50,000, 20,000, 10,000, 5,000, 1,000 and 500 (rarely used). Coins are available in denominations of 1,000, 500, 200, 100, 50 and 25, but only the larger numbers are generally used. Refuse ripped or badly worn notes as many merchants will not accept them. Change for larger notes can be unavailable in outlying areas (especially the Gili Islands) or in taxis and small shops, so break large notes in busy areas and hang on to smaller notes and coins, especially if you plan to use public telephones or transport.

ATMs

ATMs are readily available at the airport, large towns and tourist centres (except for Amed, at the time of writing) and accept major international

Indonesian Rupiah notes

networks such as VISA, MasterCard, Cirrus and Plus. Notes will generally be dispensed as Rp100,000 or 50,000. ATMs can be uncommon or unavailable in small towns and more remote areas, so plan ahead and withdraw enough cash before you travel to these places.

On Lombok, ATMs can be found in Mataram, Cakranegara, Senggigi and other large towns, but not on the Gili Islands or in Kuta.

Credit cards

Mid-range and high-end hotels, shops and restaurants in large towns and tourist centres generally accept major credit cards (usually VISA and MasterCard, less so American Express), but will usually charge a 3–5 per cent transaction fee.

Money changers

Due to numerous reported scams on Bali, money changing is less advisable than using ATMs (which offer better value anyway). If you must, banks and authorised outlets are preferable to many hotel and airport service desks, which can offer less than the official exchange rate. Use new, crisp paper currency (US notes are best), make sure no commission fee is charged, calculate the expected amount yourself (beware of being offered a rigged calculator), and carefully count your change before accepting the transaction.

Petrol is sold in bottles for motorbikes

Opening hours

Banks

Monday–Thursday 8am–2pm, Friday 8am–noon, and occasionally Saturday 8–11.30am.

Businesses (airline offices, etc.)

Generally Monday–Friday 8am–4pm and Saturday 8am–1pm, but these can vary.

Shops and restaurants

In major tourist areas, many shops will open 8am–8pm or later, and restaurants from 8am (if they serve breakfast) to at least 11pm. Places in Kuta on Bali will often stay open later, while in smaller resorts they may close earlier, especially if business is slow.

Passports and visas

Citizens of the UK, USA, Canada, Australia, New Zealand and South Africa must purchase their visa on arrival at the airport: US$10 for 7 days or US$25 for 30 days (US, Australian and Indonesian currency or MasterCard/VISA are accepted). This cannot be extended or converted into a different visa, although at the time of writing, Indonesia has future plans to offer 4-month visas. Overstays are charged at US$20 per day. Passports must be valid for 6 months from the date of entry, and proof of intended departure is officially required but seldom checked.

Pharmacies

You'll find an *apotik* ('pharmacy') in every tourist centre. They sell a wide range of medicines, but bring enough of your own prescription from home, as available dosages may be different. Seminyak has a 24-hour pharmacy located on Jalan Raya Seminyak, next to the Bintang Supermarket.

Post

Each town has a General Post Office (*kantor pos*), open during official hours (Monday–Thursday 8am–2pm, Friday 8am–noon, Saturday 8am–1pm, closed Sunday and holidays). Many towns also have independent postal agents who sell stamps and postcards and accept letters. Post boxes (*bis surat*) are small, square and orange, but are not frequently seen. Mail service on Lombok can be quite slow, so posting items from Bali may be preferable. For large or valuable parcels, international courier services such as DHL, Federal Express and TNT are available in major tourist centres and airports.

Public holidays

Indonesia has three fixed public holidays: New Year's Day (1 January), Independence Day (17 August) and Christmas Day (25 December). Muslim, Hindu, Buddhist and other religious holidays follow their own calendars and are celebrated on different dates each year. *Nyepi,* or Balinese New Year, is generally held in March or April and is also observed on Lombok. *Idul Fitri*, the Muslim celebration of the end of Ramadan, falls in October or November.

Suggested reading and media
Books
- *Bali: A Paradise Created* by Adrian Vickers – thoughtful evaluation of the complex relationship between Bali and tourism.
- *The Island of Bali* by Miguel Covarrubias – classic account by a Mexican artist of Bali's people, their lives and their culture.
- *Midnight Shadows* by Garrett Kam – historical fiction of a Balinese family caught in Indonesia's political turbulence of 1965.
- *Our Hotel in Bali* by Louise G Koke – personal account of the 1930s US couple who built Bali's first hotel in Kuta, with fantastic pictures of life in pre-war Bali.
- *A Short History of Bali* by Robert Pringle – comprehensive overview of Bali's history from ancient to modern times.

English-language newspapers
- The Bali Times (*www.thebalitimes.com*)
- The Jakarta Post (*www.thejakartapost.com*)

Websites
- *www.baliblog.com* – recommended site with a great deal of helpful information
- *www.balieats.com* – restaurant reviews, searchable by location, cuisine or name
- *www.baliforum.com* and *www.balitravelforum.com* – travellers' discussion forum
- *www.beatmag.com* – online version of biweekly nightlife and entertainment guide
- *www.indo.com* – information and discount hotel booking site
- *www.lombok-network.com* – travel information for Lombok
- *www.whatsupbali.com* – weekly listings of live music, dances and tourist sights

Tax
Tax of between 10 and 21 per cent is often added to hotel and restaurant bills, varying depending on the class of establishment. Some places will also add another 5–10 per cent for service (together referred to as 'plus-plus'). These charges should be printed at the bottom of menus and brochures. Be sure to enquire before booking a hotel, as sometimes in low season extra charges will be waived as a discount.

Telephones
Telephoning in Bali
International country codes Australia 61; Canada 1; Ireland 353; New Zealand 64; South Africa 27; UK 44; USA 1
Local directory information 108 (Bali); 106 (Indonesia)
Operator-assisted calls 100 (Indonesia); 101 (international)
To make outbound calls, look for the 24-hour, government-run *Telkom* offices, or privately owned *wartels* (usually 7am–midnight), which can be found in most tourist centres. Dial 00 +

country code + area code (minus initial 0) + local number.

Telephoning from abroad

Dial the international access code (usually 00) + country code (62) + area code (361 for most of Bali; 370 for Lombok) + local number.

Mobiles

Unlocked GSM mobile phones can be used with a local SIM chip to make domestic and international calls. These should cost approximately Rp25,000 and come with around Rp10,000 of credit (*pulsa*), which can later be topped up in varying denominations. Mobile phone stores are prevalent; look for signs that mention local services such as SimPATI, Flexi, Bebas and Jempol. International roaming may also be available from your home mobile plan, but be sure to check before your departure.

Statue with offerings, Pura Ulun Danu Bratan

Essentials

TIme

Central Indonesian Time is Greenwich Mean Time + 8 hours, or US Eastern Standard Time + 13 hours. Daylight Saving Time is not observed.

Toilets

Public toilets are few and far between on Bali and Lombok, and you may find only squat toilets without paper. Tourist sights sometimes have Western toilets and ask for a small donation for upkeep. Restaurants and hotels will have Western toilets that may be available for your use if you ask politely.

Travellers with disabilities

Although many high-end hotels are disability-friendly, Indonesia in general does not have much accommodation for people with disabilities. Pavements are often rough and sometimes broken, kerbs are high with no ramps, pedestrian crossings have no audible signals and many destinations such as temples will require climbing up and down steps.

Language

English is widely spoken in tourist centres on Bali and Lombok. The national language, Bahasa Indonesia, is quite easy to pick up, however; it is non-tonal, phonetic, written with Roman letters, and has no tenses, articles, plurals or genders to contend with.

Pronunciation

ai – as in 'w**i**ne'

au – as in 'c**ow**'

e – soft, like '**eh**' (but say selamat as 'slamat')

c – ch as in '**ch**ess'

g – always hard, as in '**g**arden'

k – hard, as in '**k**ite', except at the end of a word (such as 'banya**k**'), when it's almost silent

r – slightly rolled

Basic words and phrases

yes ya

no tidak (*with verb*)/bukan (*with noun*)

please tolong

thank you (very much) terima kasih (banyak)

you're welcome sama sama

good morning selamat pagi (*before 11am*)

good day selamat siang (*11am–3pm*)

good afternoon selamat sore (*3–7pm*)

good evening selamat malam (*after 7pm*)

good night selamat tidur (*retiring*)

goodbye selamat tinggal

see you later sampai jumpa lagi

excuse me permisi

I'm sorry ma'af

I don't understand saya tidak mengerti

how are you? apa kabar?

I'm fine kabar baik

I want... saya mau...

I don't want (it) tidak mau

I am a vegetarian saya seorang vegetarian

small kecil

large besar

cold dingin

hot panas (*temperature*)/pedas (*spicy*)

left kiri

right kanan

straight ahead terus

where? dimana?

when? kapan?

what? apa?

why? mengapa?

how much? berapa harga?

open buka

closed tutup

expensive mahal

cheap murah

near dekat

far jauh

day hari

week minggu

month bulan

year tahun

Numbers

1 satu

2 dua

3 tiga

4 empat

5 lima

6 enam

7 tujuh

8 delapan

9 sembilan

10 sepuluh

100 (200, etc.) seratus (duaratus, etc.)

1,000 (2,000, etc.) seribu (duaribu, etc.)

10,000 (20,000, etc.) sepuluh ribu (duapuluh ribu, etc.)

Days of the week

Monday Hari Senin

Tuesday Hari Selasa

Wednesday Hari Rabu

Thursday Hari Kamis

Friday Hari Jumaat

Saturday Hari Sabtu

Sunday Hari Minggu

Emergencies

Phone numbers

Integrated Emergency Response Centre 112

Ambulance 118

Police 110

Fire 113

Embassies and consulates

Most countries maintain their embassy in the Indonesian capital of Jakarta, but their consulate on Bali (there are none on Lombok) should be your first point of contact.

Australian Consulate *Jl Tantular 32, Renon, Bali.*
Tel: (0361) 241 118.
bali.congen@dfat.gov.au

Canada *Contact the Australian consulate.*

New Zealand *Contact the Australian consulate.*

South African Embassy *Jl Jend. Sudirman 28, Jakarta.*
Tel: (021) 574 0660.
saembcon@centrin.net.id

UK Consulate *Jl Tirta Nadi 20, Sanur, Bali. Tel: (0361) 270 601.*
bcbali@dps.centrin.net.id

US Consulate *Jl Hayam Wuruk 310, Denpasar, Bali.*
Tel: (0361) 233 605.
amcobali@indosat.net.id

Health risks

It's recommended to have your vaccinations (typhoid, Hepatitis A/B, tuberculosis, etc.) up to date before travelling to many parts of Asia. Talk to your doctor or check *www.mdtravelhealth.com* or your government's travel advisory website for the latest information.

'Bali Belly' is the most common ailment for Western travellers. Never drink tap water. Bottled water is cheap and readily available (use it for brushing teeth, too). Ice in restaurants is safe; it's government-regulated and made from filtered water. Be careful of spicy foods if you're not accustomed to them. If you get a stomach upset and diarrhoea, take rehydration salts and anti-diarrhoea medicine, but seek medical advice if it lasts more than a few days, becomes severe or is accompanied by fever.

Dengue fever is a risk on Bali and Lombok, and is carried by a species of mosquito different from the malaria-carrying kind. It bites during the day, so protect yourself with long sleeves and trousers or use insect repellent with DEET. Fever, headache and joint or muscle pains are the earliest symptoms, so seek medical advice immediately if you experience these after being bitten.

Malaria is not a problem in the main resort areas of Bali. It may be found in more remote parts of Lombok, especially in the rainy season, but tourist areas are not high-risk.

Sexually transmitted diseases are increasing on Bali, especially HIV.

Condoms are available in pharmacies, but it's a good idea to bring your own. **Sunburn and dehydration** are always a danger for Western travellers to the tropics. Wear plenty of high-SPF sunscreen and protective clothing, and be sure to drink plenty of bottled water.

Healthcare

Western-quality healthcare is limited here, so think twice before attempting anything that could cause real injury. There is a 24-hour pharmacy on Jalan Raya Seminyak in Seminyak, and 24-hour clinics in the Kuta area of Bali:

- **International SOS Medical Clinic**
  Jl Bypass Ngurah Rai 505X.
  Tel: (0361) 720 100
- **Legian Travellers Clinic** *Jl Benesari.*
  Tel: (0361) 758 503

On Lombok, the Senggigi Beach Hotel and Gili Trawangan's Hotel Vila Ombak have clinics.

Insurance

It's essential to get travel insurance before you leave home, as very serious accidents or illnesses will require evacuation to Singapore or your home country. Check policies carefully for coverage of medical expenses, loss of baggage, repatriation, etc., as well as for activities such as scuba diving or bungee jumping.

Crime and scams

Bali is relatively free of violent crimes, but take sensible precautions against petty thievery. Lock your luggage, keep cash and passports in a hidden money belt (not a bum bag), and keep an eye out for pickpockets, especially on local transport. Women travelling solo may get unwanted attention from local men in Bali's Kuta area and on Gili Trawangan's party nights, and it's a good idea to avoid dark alleys and the beach late at night. Narcotics use and trafficking carry heavy penalties in Indonesia (including imprisonment and death), so never buy drugs or agree to carry parcels for people you don't know. Avoid money changers as they are experts at sleight-of-hand deceptions (*see p152*).

Police

If any of your items get lost or stolen, you'll need to get a police report for insurance purposes. In remoter areas without police, such as the Gili Islands, ask for the *kepala desa* ('village head'), who will take you to the nearest police station. If you are the victim of a serious crime, contact your country's consulate. If you are driving a car or motorbike, a police officer might stop you and ask to see your international driving licence and registration papers, as well as asking for an on-the-spot 'fine' (bribe), which should be negotiated down to between Rp20,000 and Rp50,000. You are advised to hide your cash and keep only a few small notes in your wallet for show.

Directory

Accommodation price guide

Prices (usually paid for in US$) are based on a standard double room with A/C (unless unavailable) per night, not including taxes and fees. Breakfast is usually included.

★	Under $50
★★	$50–$100
★★★	$100–$150
★★★★	over $150

Eating out price guide

Prices are based on an average three-course meal for one person, without drinks.

★	Under Rp50,000
★★	Rp50,000–Rp150,000
★★★	Rp150,000–Rp300,000
★★★★	over Rp300,000

SOUTH BALI

Kerobokan

ACCOMMODATION

Villa Seri ★★

A splendid little hideaway offering impressively appointed suites and apartments with entertainment centres and kitchenettes, as well as an on-site spa, pool and Jacuzzi®, room service, and free shuttle services to Seminyak. Discount booking online.
Jl Umalas I 42.
Tel: (0361) 730 262.
www.villaseri.com

SPORT AND LEISURE

Umalas Stables and Equestrian Resort

Offers horse riding lessons and beach and rice-field tours.

Jl Lestari 9X.
Tel: (0361) 731 402.
www.balionhorse.com

Kuta/Legian/Seminyak

ACCOMMODATION

Kuta Puri Bungalows ★

Only steps from Kuta beach, with surprisingly affordable de luxe bungalows and open-air garden bathrooms. All rooms have air con, and a large swimming pool lies within the charming gardens. Advance booking advised.
Poppies Lane I, Kuta.
Tel: (0361) 751 903.
www.kutapuri.com

Mercure Kuta Hotel ★★★

Any closer to the beach and you'd be sleeping on sand. Chic-modern hotel with a spectacular rooftop pool – the perfect vantage point for viewing Kuta's famous sunsets. Junior suites available with ocean views. Discount booking online.
Jl Pantai Kuta 111X, Kuta.
Tel: (0361) 767 411.
www.mercure-asia.com

Bali Oberoi ★★★★

The last word in tranquil luxury, offering private villas with elegant Balinese décor, 24-hour room service, a full-service spa and fitness centre and beachfront pool, all set in 6 hectares (15 acres) of tropical gardens.
Jl Laksmana, Seminyak.
Tel: (0361) 730 361.
www.oberoibali.com

Legian Beach Hotel ★★★★

Large, beachfront hotel featuring mod-con hotel

rooms (some suitable for visitors with a disability) and thatched-roof Balinese-style bungalows, along with two swimming pools, a spa and massage centre, tennis/squash court and several restaurants. Discount booking online.

Jl Melasti, Legian.
Tel: (0361) 751 711.
www.legianbeachbali.com

Eating out

Warung Indonesia ★

Cheap and friendly little *warung* on a Kuta backstreet. Classic Indonesian dishes such as *nasi goreng* or *soto ayam* from as low as Rp7,000 go down well with a cold Bintang beer. Good vegetarian selection.

Gang Ronta, Kuta.

Aromas Café ★★

Recommended vegetarian restaurant with an informal café up front and atmospheric dining garden in the back. Features delicious fresh juices, salads, sandwiches and Indonesian, Greek, Lebanese, Mexican and Indian mains, plus fetching desserts.

Jl Legian, Kuta.
Tel: (0361) 751 003.

Lanai Beachbar & Grille ★★

Upscale yet laid-back lounge and restaurant with a large balcony for fantastic ocean views, featuring thoughtfully prepared mains from international cuisines, sophisticated cocktails and a sinful dessert menu.

Jl Pantai Arjuna/Double Six, Legian.
Tel: (0361) 731 305.

Tekor Bali ★★

Beachside family-friendly restaurant with a beach-hut atmosphere, serving large portions of imported steaks, pasta, pizza, fish and seafood and Indonesian dishes.

Jl Pantai Arjuna/Double Six, Legian.
Tel: (0361) 754 188.

TJ's Mexican Restaurant ★★

A local institution, serving the best Mexican food in Bali for over two decades. Large portions of all your favourites, and delicious margaritas, served in a lovely garden setting.

Poppies Lane I, Kuta.
Tel: (0361) 751 093.

Maccaroni Club ★★★

Euro-chic and stylish three-level lounge/restaurant with authentic Italian food, an extensive cocktail and wine list and nightly DJs or live performances. Free Wi-Fi for customers.

Jl Legian 52, Kuta.
Tel: (0361) 754 662.
www.maccaroniclub.com

Entertainment

Bounty Discotheque

24-hour disco housed in a replica of Captain Bligh's infamous ship. Different levels offer dance floors, bars, pool tables and a restaurant, with happy hour from 9pm to midnight.

Jl Legian, Kuta.
Tel: (0361) 754 040. www. bountydiscothequebali.com

De Ja Vu

Contemporary cosmopolitan lounge on the beach, just right for sunset cocktails. Local and international DJs spin lounge, jazz and house music. Opens from 4pm daily.

Jl Pantai Arjuna/Double

Six, Legian.
Tel: (0361) 732 777.

Double Six ('66')

A local institution, this sophisticated, all-night club on the beach road features international DJs and an open-front dance floor. Open 11pm–6am nightly; gets going around 2am.

Jl Pantai Arjuna/Double Six 66, Seminyak.
Tel: (0361) 733 067.
www.doublesixclub.com

Paddy's Pub

Boisterous, popular Aussie-Irish pub that bounced back after the 2002 bombings. Offers live music and inexpensive beer. Open 6pm–4am.

Jl Legian 166, Kuta.
Tel: (0361) 758 555.
www.paddyspubbali.com

SPORT AND LEISURE

AJ Hackett Bungy

International bungee jump company on Legian beach. Late-night weekend jumps are popular with the clubgoers at next-door Double Six.

Jl Pantai Arjuna/Double Six, Legian.
Tel: (0361) 731 144.
www.aj-hackett.com

Prana Spa & Villas

Full-service spa with beauty treatments, massage and reflexology in a lavish Indian-palace setting.

Jl Kunti 118X, Seminyak.
Tel: (0361) 730 840.
www.thevillas.net

Ripcurl School of Surf

Surfing school with classes for all levels.

Jl Arjuna/Double Six, Legian.
Tel: (0361) 735 858.
www.schoolofsurf.com

Scuba Duba Doo

PADI-certified diving school and tour company.

Jl Legian 367, Kuta.
Tel: (0361) 750 703.
www.divecentrebali.com

Nusa Dua/Tanjung Benoa

ACCOMMODATION

Conrad Bali Resort & Spa ★★★★

With a 33m (108ft) long, lagoon-style swimming pool winding gently through the grounds, a full-service spa and fitness club, daily activities, a retail village and a children's centre, this plush resort gives you little reason to want to leave.

Jl Pratama, Tanjung Benoa.
Tel: (0361) 778 788.
www.conradhotels.com

Grand Hyatt Bali ★★★★

A huge, full-service resort located near the golf course and Galleria shopping centre, featuring five themed swimming pools (one with water slide) and sleek, tasteful rooms with king-sized beds and day loungers.

Nusa Dua.
Tel: (0361) 771 234.
bali.grand.hyatt.com

EATING OUT

Ulam ★★

Just outside the South Gate of Nusa Dua is this seafood restaurant, a local favourite for fresh lobster and crab.

Jl Pantai Mengiat 14, Bualu. Tel: (0361) 771 590.

Bumbu Bali ★★★

Renowned fine-dining restaurant devoted to classic Balinese cuisine. The seven-course *rijsttafels* are particularly recommended. Also offers cooking classes.

Jl Pratama, Tanjung Benoa. Tel: (0361) 774 502. www.balifoods.com

SPORT AND LEISURE
Bali Golf and Country Club
Championship 18-hole course near Nusa Dua's main hotels.
Nusa Dua.
Tel: (0361) 771 791. www. baligolfandcountryclub.com

YOS Marine Adventures
Water sports, PADI-certified dive packages, snorkelling, boat charters and fishing.
Jl Pratama, Tanjung Benoa. Tel: (0361) 775 438. www.yosdive.com

Sanur
ACCOMMODATION
Swastika Bungalows ★
Named after the Hindu symbol for good fortune, the well-priced two-storey 'bungalows' surrounding the pretty pool here have large terraces and are just a short walk from the beach.
Jl Danau Tamblingan. 128–50. Tel: (0361) 288 693. www.indo.com/ hotels/swastika

La Taverna ★★
A wonderful hotel with a pool and elegant rooms and villas with private verandahs set in a lush

garden. The restaurant overlooking the beach is one of the best in Sanur.
Jl Danau Tamblingan 29. Tel: (0361) 288 497. www.latavernahotel.com

EATING OUT
Segara Agung ★
Delicious Indonesian and Bali fare served at tables set on the beach beneath some shady trees. Ask about times for the regular dance performances. Profits go to local charities.
Jl Dayung 43, Sanur beach. Tel: (0361) 288 446. www.segaraagung. com. Open: 8am–9pm.

Cat and Fiddle ★★
Get away from it all at this popular pub and restaurant. Order fish and chips, chicken pie or just sip a pint of beer at the bar. Live Irish music on Tuesday and Sunday nights.
Jl Camara. Tel: (0361) 282 218. Open: 7am–midnight.

SPORT AND LEISURE
Blue Oasis
An all-round sports centre at the southern end of the beach.

Everything from diving and kitesurfing to wakeboarding and yoga.
Jl Danau Tamblingan, Sanur Beach Hotel. Tel: (0361) 288 011. www. blueoasisbeachclub.com

CENTRAL BALI
Campuhan
ACCOMMODATION
Ananda Cottages ★★
Down the road from the Neka Museum, this hotel is set in large grounds amid duck-filled rice paddies, with one- or two-storey bungalows with modern baths and comfortable décor. It also features 24-hour room service, a family villa and three swimming pools. Ask about low-season discounts.
Jl Raya Campuhan. Tel: (0361) 975 376. anandaubud@denpasar. wasantara.net.id

Klub Kokos ★★
A hotel and art gallery located 1.5km (1 mile) up the river valley ridge-path from Ubud's main road. Features clean and comfortable bungalows (including a family unit), a small restaurant and a large

salt-water pool, and offers children's activities and transport around the area.

On the Campuhan ridge road. Tel: (0361) 978 270. www.klubkokos.com

Hotel Tjampuhan ★★

The oldest hotel in Ubud and formerly the estate of Walter Spies (whose house is available as a two-bedroom suite), the recently renovated Hotel Tjampuhan ranges prettily down the hillside of a river valley, and features attentive service and a full spa with jungle-grotto hot and cold pools (although the winding paths and steps might be difficult for anyone with physical challenges).

Jl Raya Campuhan. Tel: (0361) 975 368. www.indo.com/hotels/tjampuhan

EATING OUT

Nacho Mama's ★★

Slightly incongruous but decent Mexican food in the heart of Bali, with large margaritas and Martinis. Run by the owners of Naughty Nuri's up the road.

Jl Raya Sanggingan.

Naughty Nuri's ★★

An upscale expat *warung* just across from the Neka Museum, featuring fresh tuna, steaks and Indonesian and Western fare, renowned for their Martinis and regular barbecues.

Jl Raya Sanggingan.

ENTERTAINMENT

Ozigo

Bar and dance club featuring live music and local and foreign DJs. Offers free pick-up and drop-off in the Ubud area.

Jl Raya Sanggingan. Tel: (081) 2367 9736. Open: nightly from 10pm.

Ubud

ACCOMMODATION

Cendana Resort & Spa ★★

Offers spacious rooms with mod cons, large bathrooms, traditional Balinese décor and balconies overlooking the surrounding rice paddies, as well as two swimming pools, full-service spa, and yoga and meditation classes.

Jl Monkey Forest. Tel: (0361) 973 243. www.cendanaresort-spa.com

Matahari Cottage Bed & Breakfast ★★

Eccentric but full of character, this little B&B offers six fan-cooled themed rooms in different Asian styles ('Indian Pasha', 'Cinnabar Tearoom'), a pastiche Victorian-era library and social parlour, in-room massage and daily high tea.

Jl Jembawan. Tel: (0361) 975 459. www.matahariubud.com

Puri Saren Agung ★★

Ubud's palace, owned by members of its noble Sukawati family, offers several guest pavilions featuring antique furniture, four-poster beds and large sitting terraces. Amenities are simple (hot water and A/C but no TV or phone), but you can enjoy the nightly dance performances practically on your doorstep. Advance bookings required.

Jl Raya Ubud, Ubud. Tel: (0361) 975 057. Fax: (0361) 975 137.

Ubud Village Hotel ★★

This stylish yet traditional hotel offers pleasant

rooms with private gardens, king-sized beds and marble bathrooms, and a swimming pool, spa and restaurant. Packages and low-season discounts available.
Jl Monkey Forest.
Tel: (0361) 975 571.
www.theubudvillage.com

EATING OUT

Gayatri Café ★
Homey Indian-Indonesian restaurant with vegetarian options galore. Balinese buffet for two available with one day's advance notice. Also offers breakfast.
Jl Monkey Forest.
Tel: (0361) 978 919.

Bebek Bengil (Dirty Duck Diner) ★★
Beautiful garden setting with airy *bale* seating and a variety of Indonesian and Western dishes, including classic Balinese specials and attractive desserts.
Jl Hanoman, Padang Tegal. Tel: (0361) 975 489.
www.agunraka.com

Bumbu Bali ★★
Inventive Balinese, Indonesian and Indian fare, with lots of vegetarian options and even a *lassi* (yoghurt smoothie) menu. Water-garden setting has secluded *bale* tables. The chefs also offer cookery classes.
Jl Suweta.
Tel: (0361) 974 217.
www.bumbubaliresto.com

Dragonfly ★★
This cosmopolitan café features pastas, vegetarian dishes, Western, Thai and Indonesian dishes, along with live music, art exhibits, an international wine list and wireless internet.
Jl Dewi Sita.
Tel: (0361) 972 973.
www.dragonflyubud.com

Ibu Rai ★★
A spacious but intimate-feeling dining area and a large menu with Indonesian and Western dishes, including traditional Balinese desserts. Named after a well-known local artist.
Jl Monkey Forest 72.
Tel: (0361) 973 472.

Murni's Warung ★★
A four-level restaurant terraced down the valley hillside overlooking Ubud's river, featuring an extensive menu with Indonesian food, curries, lasagne, burgers, steaks, seafood and a large dessert menu.
Jl Raya Ubud.
Tel: (0361) 975 233.
www.murnis.com

Café Lotus ★★★
Beautiful views of the Pura Saraswati temple and lotus pond complement the upscale Western, Indonesian and Balinese menu. Also offers locally brewed beers from Bali's first microbrewery.
Jl Raya Ubud. Tel: (0361) 975 660. www.lotus-restaurants.com

ENTERTAINMENT

A number of different Balinese dance, puppet and music performances are offered every night at venues in and around Ubud, with free transport to and from further areas. Information and tickets are available at Ubud's tourist kiosk.
Ubud Tourist Information, Jl Raya Ubud (corner of Jl Monkey Forest).
Tel: (0361) 973 285.
www.whatsupbali.com/dance

Jazz Café

A laid-back, garden-setting lounge favoured by expats, featuring modern Asian food, an extensive cocktail list and nightly live music. Telephone for free pick-up and drop-off around Ubud.

Jl Sukma. Tel: (0361) 976 594. www.jazzcafebali.com. Open: 5pm–midnight.

Sport and leisure

Bali Adventure Tours

Offers white-water rafting and kayaking, mountain-bike and trekking trips and elephant rides. Packages include free hotel transfers, hot showers and lunch.

Tel: (0361) 721 480. www.baliadventuretours.com

Bali Sobek

White-water rafting, jungle and rice-paddy trekking, mountain-bike trips and 4WD tours. Hotel transfers included from Ubud, Kuta, Sanur and Nusa Dua.

Tel: (0361) 287 059. www.balisobek.com

Threads of Life Textile Arts Center

This gallery showcases and offers workshops on different forms of traditional Indonesian dyeing and weaving techniques.

Jl Kajeng. Tel: (0361) 972 187. www. threadsoflife.com. Open: Mon–Sat 10am–6pm.

Tabanan region

Accommodation

Puri Anyar ★

Palace homestay offering simple, traditional Balinese rooms, hosted by members of Krambitan's former ruling family. Advanced booking required.

Krambitan. Tel: (0361) 812 668. Fax: (0361) 810 885. wiryana2000@yahoo.com

Sport and leisure

Nirwana Bali Golf Course

This Greg Norman-designed course overlooks the southern coastline and Pura Tanah Lot.

Jl Raya Tanah Lot, Tabanan. Tel: (0361) 815 960. www. nirwanabaligolf.com

EAST BALI

Amed

Accommodation

Dancing Dragon Cottages ★★

Well-liked boutique hotel offering individual, *feng shui*-designed cottages with marble floors, a sleek swimming pool and a seaside restaurant that gets rave reviews for its Balinese and international cuisine.

Bunutan, Amed. Tel: (0363) 235 21. www. dancingdragoncottages.com

Santai Hotel ★★

This small hotel has traditionally decorated bungalows with lofts and garden bathrooms, set in winding gardens with an attractive pool and a restaurant overlooking the ocean.

Jl Raya Amed, Bunutan, Amed. Tel: (0363) 234 87. www.santaibali.com

Eating out

Le Jardin ★

A small, French-owned garden restaurant with nightly set dinners of Indonesian and French meals. Bookings recommended. *Babi guling* available with one-day advance order.

Lipah, Amed. Tel: (0363) 235 07.

SPORT AND LEISURE
Eco-Dive Bali

A full range of PADI courses is available, and spectacular dives for all abilities.
Jemeluk, Amed.
Tel: (0363) 234 82.
www.ecodivebali.com

Candi Dasa
ACCOMMODATION
The Grand Natia Bungalows ★

Unique hotel with koi-pond canals along an open central corridor leading to tastefully decorated Balinese rooms with private garden atriums and open-roof baths. It also has two restaurants, an infinity-edge pool overlooking the sea and low-season discounts. A real find.
Jl Raya Candi Dasa.
Tel: (0363) 420 07.
hotelnatia@yahoo.com

Bali Shangrila Beach Club ★★

A full-service resort offering small studios with kitchenettes, entertainment system and lounge area, plus wireless internet, swimming pool, spa, bar and restaurant, private beachfront, a PADI dive centre and even Balinese wedding packages.
Dusun Samuh, Candi Dasa. Tel: (0363) 418 29.
www.balishangrila.net

EATING OUT
Queen's Café ★

A pleasant little restaurant with good music and the standard fare at inexpensive prices. The set three-course menus are great value. Live music weekly.
Jl Raya Candi Dasa.
Tel: (0363) 416 55.

Vincent's ★★

This stylish lounge and restaurant near the lagoon has an elegant yet low-key atmosphere with classic jazz and cosmopolitan décor. The large European and Balinese menu features a number of meat, fish and vegetarian dishes for lunch and dinner, moderately priced and well prepared, with an international wine list.
Jl Raya Candi Dasa.
Tel: (0363) 413 68.
www.vincentsbali.com

ENTERTAINMENT
Mr. Grumpy's ★

A sports café with large-screen satellite TV, movie library, billiards, beer and wine and a bar menu. Old UK and US sitcoms shown daily.
Jl Raya Candi Dasa.
Open: until 11pm.

SPORT AND LEISURE
Sub Ocean Bali

PADI courses and dives for all levels.
Jl Sengkidu.
Tel: (0363) 414 11.
www.suboceanbali.com

Nusa Lembongan
ACCOMMODATION
Coconuts Beach Resort ★★

Very cute, A/C and fan-cooled villas spilling down a slope boasting great views over Jungutbatu beach towards Bali. Has two pools on-site; Mushroom Bay beach is a bit far away.
Jungutbatu.
Tel: (0361) 728 088.
www.bali-activities.com

EATING OUT
Linda ★

The restaurant of an excellent *losmen* run by Brits north along Jungutbatu beach, Linda serves Indonesian as well

as healthy Western fare.
Jungutbatu.
Tel: (081) 2360 0867.

SPORT AND LEISURE
World Diving Lembongan
Dive centre with courses and trips to nearly 20 dive sites around the islands.
Jungutbatu beachfront.
Tel: (081) 2390 0686.
www.world-diving.com

Padang Bai
ACCOMMODATION
Puri Rai ★
The nicest hotel in town – beachside, comfortable Balinese-style bungalows, with two pools and an excellent restaurant.
Jl Silayukti.
Tel: (0363) 413 85.
www.puriraihotel.com

EATING OUT
Café Kerti ★
This open-air restaurant up on the first floor nicely catches the evening breeze from the sea. Pick a fresh fish to be grilled or order à la carte Indonesian or international dishes.
Jl Silayukti.
Tel: (0363) 413 91.

SPORT AND LEISURE
Geko Dive
PADI dive resort and school, catering for all levels of experience. Packages available.
Jl Silayukti.
Tel: (0363) 415 16.
www.gekodive.com

Penelokan
EATING OUT
Windu Sara Jaya Hotel & Restaurant ★
This restaurant just off Penelokan's main road offers good Indonesian fare and unbeatable views of Gunung Batur, as well as no-frills hotel rooms with hot-water bathrooms and guided sunrise mountain treks.
On the road down to Kedisan.
Tel: (0366) 524 67.
windusarahotel@yahoo.com

Selat
SPORT AND LEISURE
Gung Bawa Trekking
Offers guided treks up Gunung Agung, and can arrange transportation, accommodation and food on request.
Jl Raya Songan.
Tel: (0366) 243 79.
gbtrekk@yahoo.com

Toya Bungkah
ACCOMMODATION
Arlina's Bungalows ★
Friendly little *losmen* on the main road, with clean, comfortable rooms and some hot-water bathrooms. Also has a restaurant, a guided trekking agency, and canoes and fishing equipment for hire.
Jl Raya Songan.
Tel: (0366) 511 65.

SPORT AND LEISURE
Jero Wijaya Tourist Service
Reputable agency offering guided treks up Gunungs Batur, Abang and Agung, as well as in Bali Barat National Park.
At Lakeside Cottages, off Jl Raya Songan.
Tel: (0366) 512 49.
jero_wijaya@hotmail.com

Tulamben
ACCOMMODATION/SPORT AND LEISURE
Tauch Terminal Resort ★★
This large seaside resort and 5-star PADI dive centre adjacent to the *Liberty* wreck has tasteful, comfortable rooms, family villas

(some with garden bathroom), a full-service spa, international restaurant, large pool and several different dive packages.

Tel: (0363) 229 11. www.tulamben.com

NORTH AND WEST BALI

Bedugul

SPORT AND LEISURE

Bali Handara Kosaido Country Club

The world's only championship golf course set in a volcanic crater. Also a full-service resort with three-star accommodation, restaurants, tennis courts, fitness centre and a spa. Popular with Japanese tourists.

Jl Raya Singaraja, Pancasari, Bedugul. Tel: (0362) 226 46. www. balihandarakosaido.com

Taman Rekreasi Bedugul

This recreation park offers water-skiing, parasailing, jet-skiing, motorboat or rowing boat hire and boat trips on Danau Bratan lake.

Danau Bratan, Bedugul. Open: 8am–5pm. Activity and parking charges.

Lovina

ACCOMMODATION

Villa Agung ★

UK/US-owned boutique hotel with pleasant rooms and family villas, on-site spa, cookery classes and seaside restaurant and lounge with beautiful sunset views.

Tukad Mungga, Lovina. Tel: (0362) 415 27. www.agungvilla.com

Nugraha Lovina Bay Resort Hotel ★★

This oceanfront property offers clean and comfortable rooms with cable TV, minibar and sea-view terraces, plus a large pool, on-site spa, restaurant and bar, room service and bicycle hire.

Kaliasem, Lovina. Tel: (0362) 416 01.

Rambutan ★★

Five standards of nicely furnished rooms and villas with TV and garden bathrooms, set in pleasant gardens with two free-form swimming pools. Also features a restaurant, recreational activities, children's play areas, internet and Wi-Fi, and cookery classes. Good central location.

Jl Mawar, Kalibukbuk, Lovina. Tel: (0362) 413 88. www.rambutan.org

EATING OUT

Barakuda ★

A seafood lover's delight, with extremely reasonably priced fresh squid, crabs, prawns, lobster and fish grilled to order and served with your choice of a dozen sauces. Also offers Balinese suckling pig and roasted duck by advance order.

Jl Mawar, Kalibukbuk, Lovina.

La Madre ★

A small Italian restaurant that serves pasta, meat dishes, focaccia sandwiches and other favourites, with fresh bread baked daily by the cheerful owner/chef. Tiramisu is available if ordered one day in advance.

Jl Mawar, Kalibukbuk, Lovina. Tel: (081) 755 4399.

Jasmine Kitchen ★★

A compact Thai restaurant serving excellent food and a variety of curries prepared as spicy as

you dare, with tables and couch seating on two levels.
Gang Bina Ria, off Jl Bina Ria, Kalibukbuk, Lovina.
Tel: (0362) 415 65.
Open: 11am–10.30pm.

ENTERTAINMENT
Volcano Club
German-owned bar with food, downstairs garden, pool table and televised sports, and upstairs nightclub. Busy weekends attract mostly locals and a few tourists. Look for local flyers.
Banyualit, Lovina.
Zigiz
Popular, cosy bar on Lovina's main street with mixed clientele of tourists and locals, comprehensive cocktail menu, live acoustic music every night from 8pm and football on the TV.
Jl Bina Ria, Kalibukbuk, Lovina.
Tel: (0852) 3702 9531.
www.albe.net/de/zigiz

SPORT AND LEISURE
Araminth Spa
Wellness spa offering a variety of full-body massages, reflexology, *mandi lulur* and beauty treatments.
Jl Mawar, Kalibukbuk, Lovina.
Tel: (0362) 419 01.
www.lifestylebali.com
Spice Dive
5-star PADI dive centre, with trips to Pulau Menjangan, Tulamben and other sites around Bali. Offers snorkelling, night diving, children's courses, water sports and a beachside bar and café.
Kaliasem, Lovina.
Tel: (0362) 413 05.
www.balispicedive.com

Pemuteran
ACCOMMODATION
Taman Sari ★
Lush cottages and luxury-suite bungalows (one or two bedrooms) with garden bathrooms and traditional Balinese décor, set in spacious beachfront grounds with a pool, spa, restaurant, and on-site 5-star PADI dive centre.
Pemuteran.
Tel: (0362) 932 64.
www.balitamansari.com

SOUTH AND WEST LOMBOK
Mataram/Cakranegara
ACCOMMODATION
Lombok Raya ★★
The best hotel in town, a short walk from the city centre. Rooms are quiet and have balconies overlooking either the gardens or the large pool.
Jl Panca Usaha 11, Cakranegara. Tel: (0370) 632 305. www. lombokrayahotel.com

EATING OUT
Taman Sari ★
Eat like the locals on wooden *bale* platforms surrounded by plants in this pleasant garden right next to Mataram Mall. The Lombok specialities are delicious and cheap.
Jl Raya Pejanggik, Cakranegara. Tel: (0370) 660 9599. Open: 10am–10pm.

Pemenang
SPORT AND LEISURE
Kosaido Golf Club
A beautiful 18-hole course next to the beach north of Pemenang. Has its own desalination plant. Green and caddy fee $80, equipment hire available.

Jl Raya Tanjung, Sire Bay.
Tel: (0370) 640 137/38.
siregolf@mataram.
wasantara.net.id

Senggigi and Mangsit

ACCOMMODATION

Windy Beach Resort ★
Quaint traditional
thatched cottages set in a
large and lush garden
with *bales*, restaurant and
a pool. Overlooks a
deserted beach.
Mangsit.
Tel: (0370) 693 191.
www.windybeach.com

**Senggigi Beach
Hotel ★★**
A large resort, with
bungalows and hotel
rooms set in a lovely
garden next to the beach.
It feels isolated but is just
minutes' walk from the
centre. Travel agent and
spa on-site.
Jl Pantai Senggigi.
Tel: (0370) 693 210. www.
senggigibeachhotel.com

EATING OUT

Jo's Café ★
A relaxed restaurant
along the beach, with
bales and one romantic
private sunset table
practically on the sand.
Specialities include the

barbecue fish and
tempura.
*Art Market, Jl Raya
Senggigi.*
Tel: (0370) 692 091.
Open: 10.30am–11pm.

Square ★★
A sleek and modern
restaurant with the
former chef of the
Oberoi resort cooking up
excellent steaks, sushi
and Asian fusion food.
The lounge bar upstairs
has cocktails and parties.
*Jl Senggigi Raya, Block
B10, Plaza complex. Tel:
(0370) 664 4888.*
www.squarelombok.com.
Open: noon–11pm.

SPORT AND LEISURE

Lombok Biking
Fun bicycle tours, usually
done in the early
morning. Popular rides
are from Pusuk Pass (a
minibus takes you up)
downhill to the beach,
and to Lingsar temple.
*Jl Senggigi Raya, next to
Bumbu restaurant.*
Tel: (0370) 660 5792.
Open: 8am–9pm.

Gili Islands

ACCOMMODATION

Hotel Vila Ombak ★★★
The Gilis' best hotel has

charming bungalows and
two-storey traditional
lumbung huts in a large
garden. There's a
gorgeous pool, a spa,
restaurant and beachside
bar. The resort has its
own boats from Lombok.
Gili Trawangan.
Tel: (0370) 642 336.
www.hotelombak.com

SPORT AND LEISURE

Dream Divers
A German-run diving
school offering diving
and snorkelling
excursions for both
beginner and advanced
levels. Also in Senggigi.
Gili Trawangan.
Tel: (0370) 634 496.
www.dreamdivers.com.
Open: 8am–9.30pm.

**Stud Horse Riding
Adventures**
Guided and independent
horse rides around the
island.
Gili Trawangan.
Tel: (0370) 639 248.

Kuta

ACCOMMODATION

Mimpi Manis ★
Lovely homestay run by
a UK/Indonesian couple,
with two simple but
immaculate rooms,

a house for rent and good food. A huge DVD collection is available to guests.

Jl Raya Mong, Kuta.
Tel: (0818) 369 950.
www.mimpimanis.com

Surfers Inn ★

Rooms and good-value A/C bungalows grouped around a nice pool. Near Kuta village and the beach, but set well back from the main road.

Kuta. Tel: (0370) 655 582.
lombok_hotel@yahoo.com

Novotel Coralia Resort ★★★★

A fantastically landscaped beach resort resembling a Sasak village, with thatched private villa huts and cheaper, more ordinary hotel block rooms. Spa, travel agent, dive centre and good restaurants and bars on site.

Pantai Putri Nyale, Kuta.
Tel: (0370) 653 333.
www.accorhotels.com

Eating out

Ashtari ★

On a hill overlooking Kuta, the views from this Aussie-run, shoes-off restaurant are stunning. Wonderful food; healthy breakfasts, curries, salads, brownies and coconut shakes.

Coastal road, Kuta.
Tel: (081) 7578 7502.
Open: Tue–Sun 8.30am–6pm.

NORTH AND EAST LOMBOK

Sembalun Lawang

Accommodation

Lembah Rinjani ★

A simple guesthouse with a pleasant restaurant near the RTC trek centre. Rooms are basic but clean and offer great views of the volcano.

Sembalun Lawang.
Tel: (081) 803 652 511.

Senaru

Accommodation

Pondok Indah ★

Good-value, basic but clean rooms with verandahs and fabulous views over North Lombok. Run by John's Adventures, a reliable trek agency. In the lower part of the village.

Senaru.
Tel: (0370) 639 476.
www.lombok-rinjanitrek.com

Sport and leisure

Rinjani Trek Centre

Offices of the New Zealand-funded ecotourism programme can be found in Mataram, Senaru and Sembalun Lawang. Trekking information and bookings.

Hotel Lombok Raya, Mataram.
Tel: (0370) 641 124. www.lomboksumbawa.com

Rinjani Trekking Club

A responsible trekking agent linked to the Rinjani Trek Centre, offering budget and de luxe hikes of 2–7 days, also from Aik Buka on the south flank.

Jl Raya Senggigi Km8.
Tel: (0370) 693 202.
www.info2lombok.com.
Open: 8am–9pm.

Tetebatu

Accommodation

Green Orry Inn ★

Bare but modern and clean rooms facing courtyard gardens and overlooking rice paddies. A short walk from central Tetebatu and a good base for exploring the area.

Tetebatu.
Tel: (0376) 632 233.

Index

Acknowledgements

Thomas Cook wishes to thank the photographers, picture libraries and other organisations for the loan of the photographs reproduced in this book, to whom copyright in the photographs belongs.

ALISON LEMER 14, 22, 82, 84, 90, 91, 122, 133
DREAMSTIME 89
JEROEN VAN MARLE 8, 12, 19, 25, 29, 47, 48, 49, 50, 72, 86, 87, 103, 104, 105, 106, 107, 108, 109, 110, 111, 113, 114, 119, 124, 125, 130, 135, 139, 145, 147
MARTA KARWAT 77, 134
NO ROADS EXPEDITIONS (www.noroads.com.au) 115
PICTURES COLOUR LIBRARY 1
WORLD PICTURES/PHOTOSHOT 38, 129
All other photographs were taken by ANDY DAY.

For CAMBRIDGE PUBLISHING MANAGEMENT LTD:
Project editor: Tom Willsher
Typesetter: Trevor Double
Proofreader: Karolin Thomas

SEND YOUR THOUGHTS TO
BOOKS@THOMASCOOK.COM

We're committed to providing the very best up-to-date information in our travel guides and constantly strive to make them as useful as they can be. You can help us to improve future editions by letting us have your feedback. If you've made a wonderful discovery on your travels that we don't already feature, if you'd like to inform us about recent changes to anything that we do include, or if you simply want to let us know your thoughts about this guidebook and how we can make it even better – we'd love to hear from you.

Send us ideas, discoveries and recommendations today and then look out for your valuable input in the next edition of this title.

Emails to the above address, or letters to Travellers Series Editor, Thomas Cook Publishing, PO Box 227, Coningsby Road, Peterborough PE3 8SB, UK.

Please don't forget to let us know which title your feedback refers to!